Statism, Youth and Civic Imagination

About the Author

Ebenezer Obadare is an Assistant Professor of Sociology at the University of Kansas, Lawrence, USA. He holds a PhD in Social Policy from the London School of Economics and Political Science, where he received the Richard Titmuss Best PhD Thesis Prize (2005). A MacArthur Foundation Research and Writing Grant awardee, Dr. Obadare's articles on civil society, religiosity, youth, civic service, and the state in Africa have appeared in leading journals, including *African Affairs, The Journal of Modern African Studies, Politique Africaine, Africa Development*, and *Review of African Political Economy*. In 2008, Dr. Obadare was honoured as the year's Virginia and Derrick Sherman Emerging Scholar by the Department of History at the University of North Carolina, Wilmington. He is the author of *Africa Between the Old and the New: The Strange Persistence of the Postcolonial State* (UNCW, 2008) and co-editor (with Wale Adebanwi) of *Encountering the Nigerian State: Excess and Abjection* (Palgrave, 2010).

Monograph Series

The CODESRIA Monograph Series is published to stimulate debate, comments, and further research on the subjects covered. The series serves as a forum for works based on the findings of original research. Such works are usually case studies, theoretical debates or both, but they also incorporate significant findings, analyses and critical evaluations of the current literature on the subjects covered.

Statism, Youth and Civic Imagination

A Critical Study of the National Youth Service
Corps Programme in Nigeria

Ebenezer Obadare

CODESRIA

Council for the Development of Social Science Research in Africa

Cover designed by Ibrahima Fofana
Typeset by Daouda Thiam
Printed by Imprimerie Saint-Paul

Distributed in Africa by CODESRIA
Distributed elswhere by African Books Collective, Oxford, UK
Website: www.africanbookscollective.com

Monograph Series
ISBN: 978-2-86978-303-4

The Council for the Development of Social Science Research in Africa (CODESRIA) is an
independent organisation whose principal objectives are to facilitate research, promote
researchbased publishing and create multiple forums geared towards the exchange of views
and information among African researchers. All these are aimed at reducing the fragmentation
of research in the continent through the creation of thematic research networks that cut across
linguistic and regional boundaries.

CODESRIA publishes a quarterly journal, *Africa Development*, the longest standing Africabased
social science journal; *Afrika Zamani*, a journal of history; the *African Sociological Review*; the
African Journal of International Affairs; *Africa Review of Books* and the *Journal of Higher Education
in Africa*. The Council also co-publishes the *Africa Media Review*; *Identity, Culture and Politics: An
Afro-Asian Dialogue*; *The African Anthropologist* and the *Afro-Arab Selections for Social Sciences*.
The results of its research and other activities are also disseminated through its Working Paper
Series, Green Book Series, Monograph Series, Book Series, Policy Briefs and the *CODESRIA
Bulletin*. Select CODESRIA publications are also accessible online at www.codesria.org.

CODESRIA would like to express its gratitude to the Swedish International Development
Cooperation Agency (SIDA/SAREC), the International Development Research Centre (IDRC),
the Ford Foundation, the MacArthur Foundation, the Carnegie Corporation, the Norwegian
Agency for Development Cooperation (NORAD), the Danish Agency for International
Development (DANIDA), the French Ministry of Cooperation, the United Nations Development
Programme (UNDP), the Netherlands Ministry of Foreign Affairs, the Rockefeller Foundation,
FINIDA, the Canadian International Development Agency (CIDA), IIEP/ADEA, OECD,
IFS, OXFAM America, UN/UNICEF, the African Capacity Building Foundation (ACBF)
and the Government of Senegal for supporting its research, training and publication
programmes.

Contents

Acknowledgements

This research was made possible by a grant from the Global Service Institute (GSI) of the Center for Social Development, Washington University in St Louis, Missouri, with funding from the Ford Foundation. I am indebted to several colleagues, including Dr Wale Adebanwi, Olawale Ismail, Dr Gbemisola Adeoti, Christopher Ankersen, and Dr Attahiru Jega who assisted me in various ways during the field research for the study. I also would like to acknowledge the assistance of staff at the Centre for Democracy and Development, UK, especially Dr Kayode Fayemi and Morten Hagen. My special appreciation goes to Professor Sola Akinrinade, who encouraged me at the beginning and helped in the development of the proposal for the study. For their critical comments, I am grateful to participants at the International Symposium on Civic Service: Impacts and Inquiry, held at Knight Center, George Washington University, St Louis, Missouri in September 2003. Finally, this research would not have been possible without the generosity of the entire staff of the Global Service Institute, Center for Social Development, George Washington University in St Louis, in particular Professor Michael Sherraden, Dr Amanda Moore McBride and Carlos Benitez who all assisted me greatly and provided necessary clarification at different stages of my investigation.

Introduction

This study examines the service–citizenship nexus in Nigeria using the National Youth Service Corps (NYSC) programme as an empirical backdrop. In the relevant sociological and service literature, the assumption that service is antecedent to, and necessarily impacts positively on, citizenship is a virtual axiom. However, tentative conclusions from this study provide a basis for rethinking this wisdom. Using data from open-ended interviews, questionnaires and focus group discussions, the research traces the ways in which the political dynamics in the country (Nigeria) have affected the implementation of the NYSC programme. The research concludes by articulating the conception of and prior allegiance to community as essential for the creation and nurturing of actual citizenship, and the performance of service respectively.

How is the relationship between civic service and citizenship to be understood? How does service affect citizenship? These are the two important theoretical questions that this study set out to answer. The research uses as its contextual backcloth the National Youth Service Corps (NYSC) scheme in Nigeria, which, more than thirty years after inception, seems in critical need of re-visioning. The NYSC was established in post-Civil War (1967–70) Nigeria in order to, among other things, 'raise the moral tone' of Nigerian youths, make them 'more amenable to mobilisation in the national interest', inculcate a sense of patriotism and promote national unity.

While these objectives are undoubtedly noble, the crisis that has apparently bedevilled their actual implementation has compelled a rethink of the NYSC's founding vision. This research is predicated on the hypothesis that a larger portion of the blame for this untoward situation lies in the negative political vibrations emanating from the larger Nigerian society. Other corollary assumptions are: (i) that there is a necessary relationship between service and citizenship; (ii) that youth service in Nigeria has failed to promote a sense of citizenship among the youth; and (iii) that service can enhance citizenship only within a given socio-political context.

The findings from the research would appear to validate these hypotheses. Indeed, they seem to challenge a core assumption in the relevant literature regarding the interface of civic service and citizenship. In this vein, while the usual emphasis has been on service as being antecedent to and shaping citizenship positively, this study generates conclusions that urge a conception of citizenship and a sense of community as being *prior to* the performance of service. In the case of Nigeria, it would seem that the particular shenanigans of the Nigerian state and the overall failure of governance have constituted prime impediments to the realization of any sense of citizenship, and thus the performance of service. It is suggested that this signal reversal of the service–citizenship nexus can be a useful precept in understanding not only the service/citizenship conundrum, but more broadly the crisis of the state across the postcolonial world. This is especially pertinent given the growing popularity of the idea of national service and the danger that it might be seen as the magical cure to the problem of civic withdrawal.

This is not to deny the potential of national service as a means to achieving social integration and building a trans-ethnic consciousness, especially in societies sorely tested by primordial and sectarian cleavages. If anything, this research indeed confirms the usefulness of national service in stimulating renewed faith in the *nation* project, and building bridges across cultural and ideological divides. However, this should not lead to an unalloyed faith in the agency of national service; for, as confirmed by this research, the idea is not without its own important limitations. Two of such limitations (elitism and state interests) seem particularly critical. Given the greater access that the elite have in determining, against the rule, the state, city, type of organization, etc., where their wards serve, the service programme thus has the potential of perpetuating rather than addressing unequal power and access to resources.

The other limitation is state interests, linked to elitism in that the interest of the ruling elite might frequently be camouflaged as 'state interest'. For instance, national youth service may be just a political project of giving the visage of unity or oneness to a fractured and fracturing territorial formation. In this case, while fundamental problems are not addressed, national service can be presented as a means of achieving unity, to which much lip service is paid, without any concomitant fundamental political restructuring.

To the foregoing limitations might be added the realization that national service may actually obscure fundamental problems of state, while surface-level and isolated cases of 'national spirit' and 'selfless service' may occlude confrontation with fundamental crisis and overlook them, under the guise of 'joint service to fatherland'. For instance, in the specific case of Nigeria, after thirty years of the NYSC, the country remains deeply divided, with regular inter-ethnic clashes and inter-religious clashes growing in intensity.

The key point therefore would be that, unless youth service is linked to other political and social processes of national transformation, sporadic outbreaks of patriotism and/or general tourism and sight-seeing – as some participants might cynically see service in other parts of the country – would remain its major achievement, and the transformative potential for the youth and for society would remain a mirage.

Clearly, this also has important implications for the presumed connection between the idea of service and citizenship. Anchoring its analysis in the specific emergence of the welfare state in the postcolonial world, this study affirms this linkage, but at the same time notes that service may be expected to build citizenship only when servers' faith in the joint legitimacy of the national project and the state has been assured. Thus, we may safely vouchsafe that the service-citizenship interface is contingent on other variables in the larger socio-political terrain.

Data for the study were drawn from a combination of open-ended interviews, a questionnaire survey and focus group discussions (FGDs). The questionnaires were analyzed using tables, ratios and percentages to identify trends that were subsequently elaborated upon in FGDs and interviews. Crucially, the data generated from the questionnaires were analyzed generally and proportionally with a view to understanding the similarity or divergence of opinions between serving and former corps members. This methodology has enriched the study by providing a rare, important opportunity to see the extent to which opinions and attitudes towards the programme change or are reinforced over time, especially in post-service years. Two focus group discussions (one in each of the two selected western Nigerian states of Lagos and Osun) were organized to provide insight into some of the observed trends in the questionnaires. Organizing the FGDs was logistically daunting for the primary researcher given the diverse backgrounds and occupational differences (with the implication for time and availability) of the targeted participants. The FGDs involved between eight and ten participants (who were excluded from completing the questionnaires), including serving and alumni of the NYSC. The participants were also carefully selected to reflect the diverse nature of the Nigerian nation; participants were drawn from as many different ethnic, socio-cultural, occupational and regional backgrounds. The FGDs were tape-recorded and transcribed to provide clarity and document responses.

Finally, in-depth interviews were conducted to generate further explanations, understanding and perceptions about the NYSC scheme, especially as it affects citizenship values. The target group included officials of the NYSC, serving and alumni members of the NYSC, academics and members of the civil society. Every attempt was made to ensure that the target group for the interview was not involved in completing the questionnaire and FGDs.

The Problem

The ascendancy of social anomie in Nigeria has to a large degree come to be symbolized by the younger aspect of the population. Yet this axiom is occasionally challenged by some significant actions of youth citizenship. Such actions throw up theoretical and practical challenges for the project of national cohesion (solidarity, unity and growth) and those who essay to study the dynamics of 'the social' in it. While the potential role of service in addressing the violations of the idea and space of 'the social' in postcolonial polities is often idealized and shared by many, the almost complete erosion of the same also tempers expectations that such actions that are capable of reconstructing the social space as the first condition of repairing the political space would, in actuality, be honoured or performed, if at all, by youths. It is, indeed, a paradoxical contention: normative expectations are hobbled by 'actual' expectations.

One excellent illustration of this antinomy is a story in a Nigerian national newspaper about a youth corps member who defied poor personal health and her father's opposition to serve in a 'remote' part of the country. While this very selfless and patriotic action would, at the normative level, constitute the major goal of the National Youth Service Corps (NYSC), the one-year mandatory national youth service scheme, it was seen as 'unusual' and highly commendable. The newspaper began the story, entitled 'A rare trait of patriotism', as follows: 'In these days when genuine patriots are in short supply, she (the heroine corps-member) stands out burning with love for her fatherland'[1] (parenthesis added). The newspaper reported that the lady, a sickle-cell anemia patient, 'defied her peculiar health condition, father's intimidation, threats and even physical assaults to serve in *far-away* Borno State'[2] (emphasis added).

She was rewarded at the close of her service year for 'this rare patriotism' by the Director-General of the NYSC, with the sum of ₦100,000 (about $1,000.) Instructively, the paper added that even though the lady might 'not have worked harder than her serving colleagues', what was important was that 'everyone knows that her brand of patriotism is not commonplace'[3] (emphases added) – therefore pointing to the fact that matters were not just about service, but also how.

4

That the newspaper – and invariably, the director-general of the scheme – regarded Borno State as 'far away' and the lady's action as constituting 'rare patriotism', thus contesting the social imaginary of commonality, oneness, spatial contiguity and patriotic fervour that constitute the very foundation of the scheme, reveals the deleterious effects of political dynamics within the contemporary Nigerian state on a programme that was actually designed to 'raise the moral tone of Nigerian youths'. This was to be achieved by giving them (the youths) the opportunity to learn and know more about their country and the higher ideals of service to the community – beyond the thought of reward – in addition to consolidating the corporate existence and common destiny of the people of Nigeria.

Contrast the foregoing, which can be described as a 'real-life story', with an 'official' story. Another newspaper reported that one of the state directors of the scheme in the northern part of Nigeria had pleaded for the 'naturalization' of corps members wherever they served, to 'enable them [to] become indigenes in their areas of service as a better way of enhancing unity and peaceful co-existence'.[4] Contrary to the image of 'rarity' of patriotism painted by his superior, the director-general, in awarding the lady above a prize a month earlier, the state director affirmed that the over one million youths who had participated in the scheme in the past thirty years 'have tremendously bridged the existing gap between various peoples of the nation'.[5] For this director therefore, the 'rare' – even though he offered no concrete evidence – was the 'norm'. Though his quest for 'naturalization' points to the need for better guarantees of what he described as already achieved – unity and peaceful co-existence – it is apparent that the director was convinced that the scheme had acquitted itself well. Is this therefore a case of bivalence or ambivalence?

Charles Moskos (1988:7) rightly notes that 'a civic-oriented national-service program must ultimately rest on some kind of enlightened patriotism', given that 'national service points to a civic formulation of patriotism'. Does the first narrative above, then, denote the absence of 'enlightened patriotism' and the 'civic-ness' of such patriotism? If, in the third decade of the scheme, the expected norm has become the actual 'rare', what, we may rightly ask, has become of the scheme? Again, to revisit the second narrative, if 'naturalization' is desired in order to concretize the scheme, does it (not) point to a constitutive lack in the centre of the design of the scheme and its present realities? Has the 'norm' become inadequate? Does the scheme still retain its original *raison d'être* and relevance? Going back to the first narrative, has the potential role of service in addressing the challenges – the founding ideal of the initiative – been abandoned to the 'rare'?

5

We shall proceed here, first, by offering a theoretical framework for understanding youth service and its linkage with the civic imagination and political project – in this case, national integration – in a specific context of an African postcolony, Nigeria. We will then elaborate and examine the empirical context that reflects or deflects this theoretical backcloth. This will then lead to a report of the research carried out to find out the state of affairs thirty years after the commencement of the scheme. In doing this, we are persuaded that the NYSC project is in urgent need of new data to examine its relevance and rationale in the context of the comprehensive savaging of the Nigerian idea, and the consequent loss of political and social solidarity from the second half of the 1980s, thrown into sharp relief by the upsurge in inter-ethnic and inter-faith clashes and the continued failure to build a trans-faith, trans-ethnic national ethos in Nigeria. How have the youth whose service was constructed to, and is indeed geared towards, remedying this situation, fared in the context of these overarching changes? What has happened to a major national institution – which the NYSC clearly is – for mutual comprehensibility through the agency of youth, in the context of all this?

Specifically, the key questions that we attempt to answer in this study are: What is the actual nature of the relationship (if any) between service and citizenship in Nigeria? How has politics influenced the pragmatics of service in Nigeria? Has the National Youth Service Corps (NYSC) programme enhanced civic engagement in Nigeria? Some assumptions underlie how we proceed in confronting these questions. These assumptions are tied to the key questions. First, it is assumed that there is a necessary relationship between service and citizenship; second, that youth service in Nigeria has failed to promote a sense of citizenship among the youth; third, we assume that service can enhance citizenship only within a given socio-political context.

Conceptual Framework

In general, this study variously complements, advances and, where necessary, rejects conclusions from previous studies. Three traditions of scholarship are relevant here: those relating to youth and youth policy in Nigeria, studies on citizenship both within Nigeria and internationally, and the emerging global literature on service. We shall take these sequentially and then link them up in providing a framework for the understanding of the practical context of youth, citizenship and service, which is the subject of our investigation.

Even though the crossroads of youth, citizenship and service has become central to the practice of citizenship and the gamut of civic imagination in Africa, theoretical and conceptual ways of looking at this interface are generally inadequate. The reason for this is basically found in the conceptions of youth, which, in scholarship, trump its linkage with citizenship and service. As Adebanwi (2004), following Momoh (2000:181), has noted, in Africa, youth as a social category is one of the most trivialized and oversimplified subjects of study. This trivialization and oversimplification is a derivative of the fact that for most writers and researchers, the African youth (is) a metaphor for violence and crime across the continent and therefore the analysis of the agency of youth (and the structure of the enactment of their being in society and politics) is trapped in the manifestations of violence and crime (Adebanwi 2004:8).

This author goes on to mention a few examples of this 'criminalized' conception of youth – the 'youth as hooligan' – which justifications are found in 'child' and young soldiers marching all over the beleaguered continent, and the involvement of youths in urban violence in much of the same continent.

However, while the study of youth in Africa as a 'delinquent' and 'deviant' stratum is largely over-theorized and empirically weak (ibid.), a number of studies are emerging to correct this anomaly and link youth as social category (Wyn and Rob 1997:8) with peaceful social processes that are geared towards producing and reproducing youths as citizens in contemporary African polities. Therefore, while the strong emergence of the conception of 'youth as citizen' – particularly in the conception of citizenship as duty – may not erase the empirical validity of 'youth as hooligan' in some contexts, it might at least give a balanced view of the category of youth in understanding social processes in contemporary Africa. Here, youth service is argued to constitute a model of state acculturation of the youth in the development of particular social formations.

However, existing literature on youth service in Nigeria, for instance – where the idea of institutionalized youth service seems to be most developed in the continent – would seem largely consensual. Iyizoba (1982) and Omo-Abu (1999), for example, argue that youth service promotes cultural integration. While the wisdom (or not) of aspiring towards cultural integration has been rightly debated (Eberly 1998; Sherraden 2001; Brav et al. 2002), especially against the backdrop of the mounting challenges from Nigeria's disaffected communities, it is argued here that the absence of a conception of citizenship, or the imbrication of civic imagination in these studies, raises questions about their conclusion. The theoretical departure point here links any civic attempt at promoting cultural integration with conceptions of citizenship. Existing studies, we argue, are therefore largely vitiated by their failure to come to terms with the political ramifications of youth service in Nigeria. In part, this research constitutes an attempt to provide a much-needed intellectual corrective to this situation.

Perry and Katula (2001:338) advance the view that 'there appears to be a significant gap between scholars who assert that service, by its very nature, promotes citizenship and those who argue that only particular types of service activities nurture citizen development'. This is an important divide, especially as it appears to set the stage for a further interrogation of the particular social and empirical circumstances under which service may or may not promote citizenship. It is important to insert oneself theoretically in this yet undetermined theoretical interstice. And the way to proceed is to first clear the theoretical/conceptual bushes. What is service? And what, in the context of this work, is citizenship?

1

The Idea of Service

In the emerging literature on service as a distinct social practice and analytic category, Michael Sherraden's (2001) definition has become the touchstone. Sherraden describes service as 'an organized period of substantial engagement and contribution to the local, national, or world community, recognized and valued by society, with minimal monetary compensation to the participant'.[6] Patel (2003:89) adds that service 'is shaped by the history and service traditions of a society, its level of development, the way in which it governs itself, organizes its economy and views the role of its citizens and its social institutions in meeting human needs and in promoting democracy'.

While the attempt to capture civic service in this way is recent, the idea of service itself is ancient. In a study of the etymology and historical significance of the word in several languages/traditions, Greek, Latin, Japanese, Swahili, Chinese and Sanskrit, it was found that service historically referred to 'helpful actions of individuals in relation to others' (Menon, Moore and Sherraden 2002). In these traditions, such actions, even where they manifested in different forms, were not just expressions of self-sacrifice: they were also expressive of loyalty or devotion to the state or to a higher being (ibid.).

In contemporary times, service has moved from its conceptualization in terms of individual actions and has come to be seen in terms of 'societal systems of care and governance' (ibid.:9), while ways of enacting this have become increasingly formal, institutionalized and cross-cultural. However, the way in which civic service is conceptualized is conditioned by political, ideological, economic, social, as well as cultural, beliefs in different societies (Patel 2003:92).

While Sherraden's definition focuses mainly on formal means of service participation, therefore suffering what is described as 'bias towards "developed" countries and urban centers' (Brav, Moore and Sherraden 2002:2), this bias does not limit its utility in understanding national service of the kind that the present work deals with. This is precisely because it is civic service that is neither 'urban' nor practised in a 'developed' country. Two other critiques have been made of this definition of service, which we hope to quickly dismiss in the context of this work. This is that since this is the definition of service for which there is compensation, it leaves out the voluntary or compulsory dimension of service. While one group of scholars avers that service that includes compensation of any kind would corrupt the process of service since that would not be pure 'volunteerism' (Bandow 1990; Chapman 1990), the other posits that compulsion in service undermines the freedom critical to the proper functioning of a democracy and the free market (Oi 1990).

These scholars have been countered by those who argue, in contrast to the first objection, that compensation for work that does not equal market rates does not vitiate civic service. Moreso, in the context of sustained period of national service (say one or two years), where participants – who, largely, have not been previously employed and so have no fall-back fund – take up no other form of employment and perform the service full time, there is no other means of subsistence beyond some monetary compensation. For the other objection, compulsion is a necessary condition for formal national youth service geared towards national reinvention; otherwise, the result is only a few youths who are willing to do this and therefore vitiate the goal of ensuring civic revival in the highest numbers possible.

However, laudable as this conception of service, which we happen to share, is, the literature is replete with works that assess service programmes from the departure point of the 'intentions' of the programme and a few others that consider service from the point of 'outcomes' (Brav, Moore and Sherraden 2002:3). Iyizoba (1982) and Kalu (1987), in their studies of the national youth service (NYSC) programme in Nigeria, approach from the more nuanced (Iyizoba) to less explorative (Kalu) perspectives to examine the outcomes of the programme. However, while concentrating on the benefits, they both overlook the possible harms of service, thus underestimating the negative outcomes of the NYSC.

Three major limitations to the idea of civic service, derived from similar developmental policies and programmes, have been advanced (Brav, Moore and Sherraden 2002). Two of these are relevant to this work. The first is elitism. Here, given the greater access that the elite have in determining, against the rule, the state, city, type of organization, etc., where their wards serve, the service programme thus has the potential of 'perpetuating rather than addressing unequal power and access to resources' (Ehrichs 2002, in ibid.:6).

The other limitation is state interests. Although they are not linked by Brav, Moore and Sherraden (ibid.), state interest is linked to elitism in that, some of the time, the interest of the ruling elite can be camouflaged as 'state interest'. For instance, national youth service may be just a political project of giving the image of unity or oneness to a fractured and fracturing territorial organization. In this case, while fundamental problems are not addressed, national service can be presented as a means of achieving unity, to which much lip service is paid, without any concomitant fundamental political process. This is the locus of our argument.

We should add to these limitations the idea that national service may obscure some fundamental problems, while surface-level and isolated cases of 'national spirit' and 'selfless service' may occlude confrontation with fundamental crisis and overlook them, under the guise of 'joint service to fatherland'. For instance, in the specific case of Nigeria, if after thirty years of the NYSC, the country remains deeply divided, with regular inter-ethnic clashes and inter-religious clashes growing in intensity and barbarity, what then is the effect of national service on integration, since many of those who have partaken in it are now in charge of the affairs of state?

The key point, then, would be that, unless youth service is linked to other political and social processes of national transformation, incidental cases of patriotism and/or general tourism and sight-seeing – as some participants might cynically see service in other parts of the country – would remain its major achievement, and the transformative potential for the youth and for society would remain a mirage. Our argument would therefore come down heavily on the side of those who argue that only particular types of service activities nurture citizen development. Let us briefly examine citizenship before coming to some theoretical conclusions.

2

Citizenship as Civic Duty

Citizenship is core to the idea of democratic society. Indeed, the present age is one that considers citizenship as something of cardinal significance (Heater 1999:1). Even though the idea of citizenship has become very complex, in a way reflecting the complexities of total human organization in contemporary times, two basic strands of these conceptions have become virtually hegemonic in the literature. These are the liberal and the civic republican traditions. Generally, while the one puts emphasizes on rights, the other accents duties; while the first is less demanding of the individual, the second is very demanding of the individual in his/her relationship with the state/community. These disputations are often very strong, particularly in their enactment in actual public life, thereby acquitting Aristotle (1948:1274), who wrote in *Politics* that, 'the nature of citizenship ... is a question which is often disputed' (ibid.:45). Here, we concentrate on the civic republican variant of citizenship, which underwrites the idea of civic service.

The civic republican conception of citizenship has a more venerable lineage than the liberal conception, particularly because many of the significant thinkers on the subject of citizenship adhere to this mode (ibid.:44). This veneration goes back to the Greek city-states. Even though Sparta and Athens were archetypal polarities in terms of political principles – stern authoritarianism and free democracy – instructively, both were similar in their conception of what constitutes citizenship. Riesenberg (1992:8) correctly describes Spartan citizenship as 'an intensification of the Athenian notion of public service' (Heater 1999:44–5). Though Athenians participated freely and readily in their own governance and the Spartans were more geared towards selfless devotion by citizen-soldiers, both were significant in their citizens' commitment to civic duties (ibid.:45).

The civic republican mode of citizenship posits a legal and ethical dimension of citizenship. As Dagger (2002:149) articulates it:

> Citizenship may be a matter of legal status that confers various privileges and immunities on the citizen, in other words, but it must be more than that. 'Real' or 'true' citizenship requires commitment to the common good and active participation in public affairs. It requires civic virtue.

While this mode does not deny the legal status of citizenship, it emphasizes that although this is a necessarily condition of citizenship, it is insufficient for 'real' or 'true' citizenship. What makes citizenship 'full', 'true' and 'real', therefore, is the ethical dimension, which draws from the Greek and Roman heritage of *civitas* and *polis*, where citizens were not only entitled to participate in civic affairs, but were expected to do so (ibid.:149). The need to distinguish between 'good' and 'bad' citizens, the standards that are built into the conception of citizenship, are therefore regarded as a function of this ethical strain, and not the legal condition.

The public nature of this strand of citizenship manifests in two basic ways: public spirit and civic involvement. Consequently, a citizen in this context is one who places the public interest above his personal interests by discharging his public responsibilities and one who is also committed to the public good through civic involvement (ibid.:150). Alexis de Tocqueville suggests that anyone whose citizenship manifests in the two basic ways above is also likely to become a better, more virtuous person in other respects. This immediately points to two further dimensions of the civic republican notion, which are the integrative and the educative. In the integrative dimension, as Rousseau advances, private interests are set aside and the only interest that matters is the interest of the individual as member of the public. The individual integrates his various roles into the role of 'citizen as member of the public' and s/he also integrates her/himself into the community (ibid.:150–1). In the educative dimension, the active citizen educates and is educated about drawing out abilities that might remain untapped or unfulfilled and which will prove valuable even in other respects of the citizens' lives (cf. ibid.:151).

Heater (1999) provides a succinct typology of the purpose, style, quality, role and process of forming the citizen under the civic republican tradition (see Table 1). In this typology, the purpose of citizenship is to connect the individual with the state in a symbiotic relationship that creates a just and stable republican polity in which the individual enjoys freedom (we will return to this in linking duties and rights in this conception). Freedom is possible for the individual only in a republic, and the republic also exists through the support of its citizens. Freedom here, however, following Rousseau, denotes 'civil liberty as freedom through the merging of self-interest with duty' and not 'natural liberty as freedom through the pursuit of interest' as in the liberal conception (ibid.:53).

Table 1: Civic Republican Tradition of Citizenship[7]

Purpose of Citizenship	Freedom; republican state
Style of Citizenship	Community – friendship, concord, fraternity; issue of property
Quality of Citizenship	Virtue, patriotism, judgment
Role of Citizenship	Civil and military duty/participation; watch in government
Forming the Citizenship	Problem of motivation, education, religion

In terms of the style of citizenship, the republican mode emphasizes fundamentally the necessity of state and citizens to be a community, an 'organic society' and not merely a collection of individuals. While constitutions and laws lay down the rules by which individuals live in a state, they are not able to make communities, as they constitute only 'the propitious conditions in which a group can gel into a community'. The real 'gelling process requires the essential ingredients of social friendship and harmony' (ibid.:55), which constitutes expressions of real community.

The Greeks believed that there are four particular forms of goodness, which have become intrinsic to the qualities of citizenship of the republican mode. These are: temperance, justice, courage and wisdom, and prudence. These, it can be argued, have come to be largely, even if not wholly, fused in the modern concept of patriotism. This concept, rooted in the idea of the citizen-soldier, which Machiavelli believed was the product of military training and religious indoctrination, presages the ultimate sacrifice for one's country (ibid.:60). In modern terms, the citizen-soldier is the citizen-patriot, whose patriotism is the product of the state's cultivation (cf. ibid.:60–1). Argues Heater:

> This patriotism … has to be constantly refreshed through the virtuous mores of the community and, particularly, through the messages transmitted by the civil religion which Rousseau thought so essential for the political health and success of the state. Machiavelli also believed that religion, and more especially military discipline, was required to keep up the patriotic spirit (ibid.:61).

It is clear therefore that central to this conception is the idea of martial training both of the body and of the mind, given its implication not only in the cultivation of the citizen, but in the more crucial, even if latent, duty of the defence of the state. Again, this points to the fact that the individual-as-citizen in this mode exists for the collective/state and not to gratify the self; the citizen has meaning and significance only as s/he is attached and linked to the state by *sacrifice*.

The citizen's roles are also very vital. In fact, in this mode, the citizen is a soldier as well as an administrator in that s/he is a partaker in the governance of the state and a defender of its integrity. As Heater captures it, 'no duties, no republic'. If citizens are unwilling to fight for the republic, 'it will be overwhelmed by its external enemies; and if citizens are unwilling to contribute to the civil affairs of the republic, it will collapse into corruption and dissension' (ibid.:64).

In terms of forming the citizen, the republican tradition is supremely exacting. In fact, what it demands is 'unquestioning loyalty and total sacrifice' (Dagger 2002:150), described as 'scarcely a natural human activity' because 'it requires the acquisition of knowledge and the development of skills; it requires considering the interests of others, not just one's own, even preferring them' (Heater 1999:65). But Rousseau argues that the 'General Will', where it prevails, precisely ensures that the will of all is identical with the interests of the parts. He therefore advocates a civil religion comprising 'sentiments of sociability, without which it is impossible to be either a good citizen or a loyal subject' (ibid.:68).

However, from the late eighteenth century on, the republican mode of interpretation of citizenship gave way to the liberal mode. Nonetheless, the republican conception has witnessed a revival since the later decades of the twentieth century, given what many perceived as the inherent weaknesses of the liberal mode and the consequent 'degeneration' of community feelings and loyalty to the state in the emergent world. There are many ways in which this mode is being re-enacted, rearticulated and remade in its reappearance. One that is significant for this work is the reappearance of the citizen-soldier in the form of the mobilization of young people through paramilitary or civilian structures for participation in communal and/or national service.

Although not so posited in the literature, we argue that the emphasis on duty as the more crucial aspect of citizenship advanced by the republican conception, even where it understates rights, actually emphasizes rights in a roundabout way. The imperative of duty and participation in state and society necessarily implies a strong commitment occasioned by the right of membership. This right, therefore, always already carries the rights de-emphasized by the rhetoric of the republican conception; yet this right is conditional on duties to the whole (the state/community), which in turn rest on the rights of membership. Andrew Heywood (1994 :187) essentially supports this reading when he states that citizens are not merely bearers of rights, but that 'they also have duties and obligations towards the state that has protected, nurtured and cared for them'.

Yet, it must be noted that this conception of citizenship, which supervenes the idea of civic service – particularly of the compulsory variant, like the National Youth Service schemes, but also, of the more structured, institutionalized and formal ones, say the United States Peace Corps – has important limitations. The more crucial aspects of these limitations are the assumptions that are built into it. First, it is assumed that the state and the citizens are engaged in a common project and process of state/nation-building, in which all are demonstrably devoted and invested. Second, related to the first or enfolded in it, is the assumption that the effects of this common or joint venture are evident at every stage of the process, thereby renewing and revalidating the ideal or/and the target – state consolidation and nation-building through national solidarity and development.

The third assumption is that the only legitimate means of public participation is as a citizen-soldier involved in the defence of the state – or in contemporary times, citizen-civilian involved in sacrificial communal or national service – and one who participates directly in governance. This restrictive definition consequently is capable, in given contexts, of trivializing social engagement and relegating crucial forms of citizenship enactments such as those, as pointed out by Heater (ibid.:73) of pressure groups, trade unions and charities.

The first two assumptions overlook the clear incongruence that exists in particular societies/states between the wishes of the larger majority of the people and the actual constitution of the state. This is because the state is assumed, *a priori,* to have been produced by common consensus. In multi-ethnic, multi-religious and often fractious states where dissonance exists at many levels (of which Nigeria is a prime example), these assumptions and the consequent emphasis on duties above rights may be problematic. In such contexts, the more crucial service to the state – as enacted by pressure groups, trade unions and other civic groups – may in fact lie more in reconstituting the state than consolidating it. Since these assumptions and their implications already speak to the linkage of service and citizenship, we will draw some theoretical conclusions here by offering a word on this linkage.

3

Interfacing Service and Citizenship

Civic service is predicated on the assumption that service is a positive influence on citizenship. Perry and Katula (2001:336) point to Azaro's (1993) important observation on national service that, 'An ideal, either implicit or explicit, of active citizenship can be found as a constitutive element in every theory or proposal for national service.' Explicitly, then, change towards, or consolidation of, active citizenship is the goal of service. This, as Perry and Katula (2001) advance, is predicated on five factors: antecedents, attributes of service, attributes of the server, individual changes, and institutions (336).

Antecedents, which Verba et al. (1995) identify with four generational processes beginning from infancy – including parental education and the socioeconomic path to political activity/political socialization in the home/community roots/parental-respondents' church attendance and community roots – are not necessarily deterministic, but they raise two critical questions on the service–citizenship interface (Perry and Katula 2001:337–8). One is to what extent service may be regarded as an efficient and effective method for either modifying or reinforcing the strong dynamics that operate between generations.

The second of Perry and Katula's factors is how service can be instrumental as a change mechanism. In terms of attributes of service, there is a debate among those who assert that service, by its very nature, promotes citizenship, those who state that only particular kinds of service promote citizenship, and those who question the very idea that service promotes citizenship (ibid.:338–9). Individual differences such as age and social class are also taken to be a factor in terms of how service influences citizenship. There are also individual changes, such as intellectual stimulation, socialization and practice, which impact on citizenship. Institutional filters, such as local communities, national political systems, schools, etc., can also be viewed as antecedents of service and therefore as filters for the effects of service on citizenship. The latter is crucial because:

institutions ... provide understandings about prescribed behavior, and implicit and explicit principles or norms around which actors' expectations converge. In this capacity as rule-defining and rule-enforcing mechanisms, institutions can magnify or attenuate the effects of service on citizenship (Perry and Katula 2001:340).

Of the various theoretical approaches to understanding civic service – including philanthropy, institutionalism, conservative, critical and social development approaches – a modified version of institutionalism would fit the civic republican conception of citizenship in explicating here the service–citizenship interface. Curiously, this fitting framework is based on the liberal tradition, which the republican conception of citizenship counterposes. An attempt at theoretical purism often vitiates the power of analysis, where nuances are often transgressed in order to keep to 'the picture'. In understanding the particular account of national service that we wish to render here, marked as it is by such dissonance, the matching of a liberal concept of service with a republican notion of citizenship would render the account more open to analysis. Why is this so?

The observed conceptual complex is a mixed one. Buoyed up by the nature of the welfare state in developing countries, particularly in the African postcolony, which invested heavily in the idea of public spending to develop the emergent states and create national progress and unity, a strong conception of citizens who owe the state every duty was concomitantly developed. Consequently, the state promotes values of altruism, social solidarity and collectivism, which underpin institutional thinking (Patel 2003:93), which are backed by extensive state spending characterized by strong service delivery by the state (ibid.). As Patel argues, 'civic service programs in these types of political and social systems would tend to be more institutionalized in the form of public policy and the regulation of such activities' (ibid.). She then adds a very illuminating comment about the fact that 'the impact of institutional approaches on civic service in the developing world appears to be limited due to the weakness of the state and democratic institutions, civil conflicts (and) fiscal constraints…' (ibid.:94).

Yet, even in this developing context, the idea of service as an essential means of making citizens of the youth is so crucial that, even where it is afflicted by the problems noted by Patel and more, the 'ideal' is still romanticized and promoted given that it is also crucial to the social and political imaginary in these states, which are mostly plagued by centrifugal forces. Youth service and citizenship are linked in such contexts where, to use Youniss and Yates' (1997:17) words, 'service is a means to form citizens who understand the struggle and rewards, energy and exhilaration, that make up the actual political process' of the struggle for national unity and progress.

20

4

The NYSC: History and Rationale

If Nigeria is to make rapid progress on all fronts internally, and if she is make her mark on the continent of Africa, and indeed, in the comity of nations, her youths must be fully mobilized and be prepared to offer willingly and without asking for return, their best in the service of their nation at all times.[8]

Background

Faced with a total breakdown of social harmony following Nigeria's thirty-month Civil War (1967–70), which followed the unsuccessful attempt by the then Eastern Region to secede from the country, the then Federal Military Government (FMG) realized that having won the war, it was imperative that the peace – of solid and voluntary national unity – be won. It was a clear realization that, even though the constituent parts of this multi-ethnic and multi-religious country have been forced to *stay* together – as they were forced in 1914 by the British to *come* together – true feelings of loyalty and solidarity that produce national cohesion and unity upon which national progress and growth are predicated could only be an outcome of a deliberate social process.

This, more or less, parallels Williams James's statement in his famous 1910 essay, 'The Moral Equivalent of War', that 'national service present(s) a means by which a democratic nation could maintain social cohesion without having to go to war' (Moskos 1988:9). For a country that had already gone to war, the way to avoid another relapse into the ugly past was to engineer 'new citizens' united in common allegiance to the nation-state through service. Given the absence of a common ancestry and common national mythologies providing the primordial loyalty upon which nations are often based, national cohesion in Nigeria has to be based on some civic ideal (cf. Moskos 1988:9) or national imaginary.

The challenge that Nigeria, with an estimated 374 ethnic groups, faced in the immediate post-Civil War period therefore was how 'to engage in deliberate social engineering, designing programs and pursuing policies meant to promote national unity, de-emphasize points of discord amongst the constituent groups, and foster greater inter-ethnic understanding and harmony' (Enegwea and Umoden 1993:2). The citizenship and youth training scheme in Nigeria, dubbed the National Youth Service Corps (NYSC), was developed against this backdrop.

The fact that the programme was specifically targeted at 'youths' points to the fact that the emergent nation-state was investing in its future, particularly in the context of the unsavoury past. As was recognized at the start of the programme, 'youths constitute a dominant force for national mobilization and growth and as such, have a crucial role to play in the all important task of nation-building'.[9] Incidentally, the calls for youth service that presaged this scheme germinated in the very ambience of hostilities.

Initially, many youth groups asked for a national youth scheme beginning with provision of relief to the war-damaged and eventually evolving into a permanent agency for national mobilization (ibid.:9). With the end of the war in sight in 1969, the Committee of Vice Chancellors (presidents of universities) called for the institutionalization of a one-year national service scheme for undergraduates after the completion of their first year to 'inculcate the spirit of service and patriotism' and to promote national unity (ibid.). This soon became the subject of a major national debate in Nigeria.

At the close of the war, as the first head of the NYSC averred, it became abundantly clear to discerning observers of the Nigerian political scene that to build enduring national unity, Nigerian youths from all ethnic groups (a) ought to be mobilized and put in the forefront of the task of nation-building and integration; and (b) patriotism, dedication to the Nigerian nationhood and mutual respect for and understanding of the different ethnic groups and constitute the people of Nigeria (Adedeji n.d.:20). The military head of state, General Yakubu Gowon, following the cessation of hostilities, announced in a spirit of magnanimity that there was 'no victor, no vanquished' in the war, and consequently embarked on a programme captured as the 'Three Rs': Rehabilitation, Reconstruction and Reconciliation.

As Iyizoba (1982:3) describes it, 'in the interest of fostering national unity, the Nigerian government sought to ease the tensions and animosities among the tribal groups by creating a national unity that would supersede ethnic and tribal loyalties and weaving a spirit of nationalism among groups whose relations were traditionally antagonistic'. In the context of this, Gowon proposed that two national youth schemes, one voluntary and the other compulsory, be established.

History and Rationale

However, the government eventually decided on only the compulsory national youth service with the promulgation, on 22 May 1973, of the National Youth Service Corps (NYSC) Decree 24 of 1973, 'with a view to the proper encouragement and development of common ties among the youths of Nigeria and the promotion of national unity' (Enegwea and Umoden 1993:10–11). It is therefore clear from these statements that the overriding *raison d'être* of service here was not essentially about the intrinsic value of service, but about what service could do, that is, what resulted from the process of service. Yet, it is interesting that in the official objectives of the scheme as contained in the enabling legislation, the latter was secondary, while the former constituted the primary goal of the scheme. Indeed, only one of the objectives was explicit on this key goal of national unity. What may be deduced from this is that the other objectives were expected to key into this overriding basis of the scheme, given that as crucial ways of producing active citizens their end result would be the promotion of national unity.

The objectives of the scheme as contained in section 1 (3) of the enabling legislation were:

a. to inculcate discipline in Nigerian youths by instigating in them a tradition of industry at work and of patriotic and loyal service to the Nation in any situation they may find themselves;

b. to raise the moral tone of our youths by giving them the opportunity to learn about higher ideals of national achievement and social and cultural improvement;

c. to develop in our youths attitudes of mind, acquired through shared experience and suitable training, which will make them more amenable to mobilization in the national interest;

d. to develop common ties among our youths and promote national unity by ensuring that:

   (i)   as far as possible youths are assigned to jobs in states other than their states of origin;

   (ii)   each group, assigned to work together, is as representative of the country as possible;

(iii)   the youths are exposed to the modes of living of the people in different parts of the country, with a view to removing prejudices, eliminating ignorance and confirming at first hand the many similarities among Nigerians of all ethnic groups;

e. to encourage members of the service corps to seek, at the end of their corps service, career employment all over the country, thus promoting the free movement of labor;

f. to induce employers, partly through their experience with service corps members, to employ more readily qualified Nigerians irrespective of their states of origin; and

g. to enable Nigerian youths to acquire the spirit of self-reliance.

Eligibility for the one-year service under this scheme according to the NYSC Decree 1973 included any Nigerian citizen who (from the inception of the pro-gramme in the 1972–73 academic session) shall have graduated from a univer-sity in Nigeria or (from the 1973–74 academic session) outside Nigeria, or (from the 1975–76 academic year) shall have obtained the Higher National Diploma (HND) or the National Certificate of Education (NCE) or any other professional qualification as may be prescribed. The thirty years' age limit removed in 1977 was restored by Decree No. 21 of 1985, which amended this instrument. At inception, the service was compulsory for those who were thirty years old and below, but voluntary for those above thirty. The 1985 amendment also removed holders of the NCE from the list of eligible corps members.

In pursuance of the 'objectives of forging unity, integration and inter-ethnic understanding', corps members are posted to states other than their own and outside their cultural boundaries to ensure that the corps members (popularly called 'corpers') 'learn the ways of life of other Nigerians, and imbibe a more liberal outlook in preparation for their role as future leaders of this country' (Enegwea and Umoden 1993:15). As Enegwea and Umoden note, in all these, one major objective of the scheme, which is often ignored, perhaps because it is not expressly stated in the enabling instrument, is that of raising:

a leadership class of which the country can be genuinely proud, a class amongst the educated youth which is patriotic, morally and physically disciplined and truly nationalistic. The members of this class, having gone through the triple liberating experience of higher education, na-tional service and exposure to other cultures, would then act as change

24

agents, social catalysts to take the county to the Promised Land of Unity (Enegwea and Umoden 1993:4, emphases added).

The 'triple process' is expected to liberate the informed and cultivated individual (through higher education), the dutiful citizen-patriot (through national service) and the nationalistic subject (through exposure to other cultures) ostensibly lurking in the Nigerian youth towards the actualization of a national imaginary, which Enegwea and Umoden (ibid.) describe as the 'promised land of unity', or what others are wont to describe as 'Nigeria's manifest destiny'. Central to this is the idea of youth as symbol of hope for the future (Giroux 1996, in Youniss and Yates 1997:4) and supervening this 'triple process' is the idea enunciated by Moskos (1988:7) that every 'civic-oriented national-service program must ultimately rest on some kind of enlightened patriotism'. *The Guardian*, a Nigerian newspaper, was therefore succinct in an editorial when it described the overall goal of the scheme as the development of 'an educated, nationally oriented Nigerian citizenry'.[10]

The scheme consists of four phases: Mobilization; Orientation; Primary Assignment and Community Development Service; and Winding up Activities and Passing-Out-Parade. The key fields to which corps members were to be deployed, as mentioned in the enabling decree, included hospitals, farms, water-schemes, road construction, surveying and mapping, social and economic services, schools, food storage and pest eradication, rehabilitation centres, sports development, government departments and statutory corporations, development projects of local councils and the private sector of the economy (Iyizoba 1982:4). Initially, the service was divided into primary and secondary assignments. For the primary assignment, each of the corps members was deployed to perform his national service in a field relevant to his qualification. The secondary assignment takes four weeks and involves mobilization in groups to perform community and rural development in various locations (ibid.).

A three-week orientation programme, 'designed to give corps members a proper understanding of the scheme's goals and ensure that they internalize its ideals' (Enegwea and Umoden 1993:53) is the first phase of the programme, and consists of citizenship and leadership training, which are in two parts, drill and non-drill. The non-drill activities were initially provided by instructors from the Citizenship and Leadership Training Centre, including such activities as rope climbing, rock scrambling, adventure trips, solo survival schemes, swimming, canoeing and first aid. The Army is in charge of the drill activities. At inception, the corps members expected the drilling to include some elementary military training, but were disappointed. Three decades after, commentators still demand military training for the corps members. As one former participant in the scheme articulates it, 'there should be greater emphasis on military training as a sort of countervailing force against future coups'.[11]

However, it did not come as a shock that a deeply politicized military that was intent on monopoly of political power, which partly depended on a tamed citizenry, would be reluctant to encourage dispersal of knowledge of, and training in, weaponry systems even of the most elementary forms. Even the first head of the programme, an academic, had stated that he could not understand why the Federal Military Government (FMG) refused flatly to include basic military training in the drill activities, but he suspected that it could be because 'it was thought that this would give the NYSC products countervailing power *vis-à-vis* the military administration' (Adedeji, n.d.:30).

Furthermore, initially, the orientation programme included a series of lectures on the history, politics and administration, economics and ideology of Nigeria. While this would serve as further knowledge for those who were graduates of the social sciences and were therefore already familiar with these matters, it constituted a broadening of knowledge for the majority of the corps members who were not from a social science background. The lectures were to emphasize national unity and nation building, our common heritage in spite of our diversity, the emerging ideology of Nigeria, continuity in the aspirations of Nigerian leaders and people, the growing significance of the public sector and its control of strategic economic sectors … and the special position of Nigeria in the Black World (Adedeji, n.d.:30–1, emphasis added).

The lecture programme was to be rounded off by examining the role of the Nigerian Youth in

> (a) promoting national unity and integration; (b) accelerating the pace of economic and social development; (c) improving the physical environment of Nigeria; and (d) promoting the mental and spiritual de-colonisation of Africa and the Black World (ibid.:31).

Reactions

In spite of the fact that many youth organizations had called for the setting up of a national youth programme to provide relief during the war, which was expected to evolve into a more permanent agency of national mass mobilization (ibid.:9) and that university students at Ibadan, Ife, Lagos and Zaria also craved to be conscripted into the armed forces during the war (Adedeji n.d.:20), when the NYSC was announced in 1973, there was strong opposition to it (Enegwea and Umoden 1993:15). University students were in the vanguard of this opposition, which was worsened, according to Enegwea and Umoden (ibid.), who wrote an official history of the scheme in its twentieth year, by the absence of a 'comprehensive program of enlightenment designed to sell the scheme to the students and to promote a general understanding of its nationalistic purpose to the populace'.

While this might be plausible, we like to observe that the tendency to ignore the importance of consultations with core constituencies that will be affected by particular official programmes is an attitude native to government in Nigeria. There is often the presumption that since the government (even the illegitimate, military regimes) is supposed to represent the people and 'knows better', particularly on a matter that is geared towards national unity, everyone ought to fall in place. It is in the character of the state that tramples over civil society to assume that civil society would understand that every action of the state is in the best interest of the people. That there was no 'enlightenment programme' could be seen as another manifestation of this mindset.

The ensuing protests, which started with lecture boycotts, later took a violent turn as the university students rioted around the country, leading to a temporary closure of some of the universities (Iyizoba 1982:72). University of Ibadan students, for instance, set government vehicles on fire to register their opposition to the programme.

Specifically, students and their parents/guardians were wary of the scheme for four critical reasons. First was the disappointment of parents and their wards that after investing so much in them, the new graduates would not be able to join the labour market and so either pay back their investment by assisting the family or at least relieving the family. Some therefore argued that such a scheme should have been preceded by free university education.[12] Secondly, the students were opposed to what they considered less than-subsistence-level remuneration (called allowances) to be paid monthly.[13]

The third objection was a reflection of one of the very facts of national life that the scheme was designed in part to address – the regional divide.

Students and social commentators in the south of the country complained that the scheme was another evidence of how the Nigerian state was captive to the interests of the 'north'; and given that participants were supposed to serve in states other than their own, the scheme, it was believed, could only have been designed to address the serious manpower crisis in the less-developed northern part of the country. The north was educationally disadvantaged, therefore most of the potential participants would be from the southern states. The fact that the disadvantaged were actually more in need of service than those who had advantages and that such a gesture of assistance to the north led by young citizens from the south would help to cement national solidarity had little value for those making this argument.

The last core objection was that most parents did not want their wards to serve in places 'far away from home' (ibid.:16). This fear was heightened by two factors. One was the scary narratives of the 'bestial' and/or 'evil spirit-filled' 'Other' that pervaded (and regrettably still pervades) inter-ethnic relations in Nigeria. The other is that since the war, which ended only less than three years earlier, was preceded by a pogrom in the north of Nigeria (specifically against the Igbo), no one was absolutely sure that it would not happen again. As it happened, these fears were precisely what again reaffirmed the need for the scheme. The government therefore went ahead in spite of the reservations and fears, compelling the 'youths (to) obey the Clarion call'[14] of the Head of State to contribute 'their essential quota to the realization of our national objective of building a strong, united and self-reliant nation' (ibid.:74).

The pledge that every corps-member reads speaks to the lofty goals of the citizenship/service interface that necessitated the scheme. Each corps-member affirms that 'in pursuance of *our* aspiration to build a united, peaceful, prosperous, hate-free, egalitarian society and a great nation and of our motto 'Service and Humility' (ibid.:22, emphasis added), s/he would, among others:

> (i) at all times and in all places think, act, regard myself and speak first as a Nigerian before anything else; (ii) be proud of the fatherland, appreciate and cherish the culture, traditions, arts and languages of the nation; (iii) be prepared to serve honestly, faithfully and, if need be, pay the supreme sacrifice for the fatherland; (iv) see myself always as a leader who must give effective leadership by my transparent honesty and selfless service; etc.[15] (Iyizoba 1982:22–3, emphasis added).

The fact that corps members are compelled to affirm 'our aspiration' in the pledge is to join him/her with others in a national imaginary, which is then fleshed out in the lists of what the 'server' will do to accomplish this aspiration, including paying the supreme price, which ordinarily is expected of the citizen-soldier. At the normative level, therefore, the citizen-'server' is also a citizen-soldier.

28

5

The Development of the NYSC

In looking back at the rationale for the national youth programme, the man who set it up, General Yakubu Gowon, stated twenty-one years later that the goal was to set up:

> an enduring scheme for the edification of our youth, which would offer them the opportunity to learn and know more about their country and the higher ideals of service to the community beyond the thought of reward. We also saw it as an abundant source of high-level manpower to be put to the service of the nation and the community.[16]

The scheme started with 2,117[17] members in 1973, expanded to 46,685 in the first decade and over 50,000 in its second decade (Enegwea and Umoden 1993:25). In its third decade, it now boasts of 85,000 members.[18] This phenomenal increase in the number of participants, coupled with the need to address emergent lapses and reassess the programme, have necessitated some changes in the structure of the scheme.

Currently, the four steps of the service year have been refined. The orientation course is designed to give corps members:

> a proper understanding of the scheme's goals and ensure that they internalize its ideals. It is also designed to familiarize them with their new environment, prepare them for their unique roles during the service year as well as instil discipline, inculcate the spirit of national consciousness and promote a sense of collective responsibility and *esprit de corps* among all members (Enegwea and Umoden 1993:53-4).

Last but not the least, the orientation is also geared towards giving corps members 'adequate physical and mental training and equip them with practical, social and leadership skills to enable them meet the varied challenges of the service year' (ibid.:54). This phase comprises the swearing-in ceremony where the oath is taken, general orientation, professional orientation and passing-out parade. Primary assignment and community development, which came after the one month (later three weeks, now two weeks) of intensive training, constitute the two most important and demanding aspects of the scheme.

Primary assignment is carried out in a specific institution, either in the public or private sector. This is where the corps-member is to serve the length of the year. Community Development Service (CDS), in which the corps-member participates once every week, away from his/her place of primary assignment, involves 'projects aimed at harnessing the skills, creativity and innovativeness of the youths into effective machinery for national development and is discharged to the corps member's host community' (ibid.:56). It used to be concentrated in a six-week programme, but is now all-year round. Its objectives, among others, include:

a) Harnessing the knowledge and skills of corps members into an effective machinery for achieving self-sufficiency in the priority areas of food production and provision of agro-based raw materials for industry, economic recovery and self-reliance;

b) Providing on-the-job training and experience for corps members in the areas of Health, Engineering, Agriculture, Education and Social Services, among others;

c) Providing a forum for corps members to experiment with ideas and translate them into concrete achievements towards national development; and

d) Developing the spirit of entrepreneurship in corps members thus de-emphasizing dependence on public service employment and promoting self-employment ventures (Enegwea and Umoden 1993:57).

This phase of the programme is crucial because it taps into the practices in traditional African societies in their regular resort to meeting common challenges through common efforts (ibid.:59). This practice of practical communal work to build communities and confront communal challenges from road networks to traditional physical infrastructure, which has been eroded by urbanization and modernization, was reconstructed and injected into the scheme.[19]

Hope and Despair

If one takes account of the statements of the heads of the Nigerian state over the years, in terms of their charge to the corps members and assessment of what the scheme is capable of doing and has done, one could come to the conclusion that

30

the scheme has been an unqualified success. 'The purpose (of the scheme)', said the founding head of state, Yakubu Gowon, in June 1973:

> is primarily to inculcate in Nigerian youths, the spirit of selfless service to the community and to emphasize the spirit of oneness and brotherhood of all Nigerians irrespective of cultural background. The history of our country since independence has clearly indicated the need for unity amongst all our people... (Enegwea and Umoden 1993).

About a decade later, President Shehu Shagari confirmed that the hope expressed by Gowon had been achieved, stating that:

> participants of the NYSC have continuously made us proud and have justified the optimism of the founding fathers of the corps scheme. The discipline, the dedication to duty and loyalty they displayed each succeeding year, and their general comportment have been very admirable... (Enegwea and Umoden 1993).

The general who upstaged the Shagari-led democratic government did not share this optimism. For Muhammadu Buhari, speaking to the corps members in July 1984, the scheme's value lay in its potential and not in what it had achieved. Thus,

> Members of the NYSC constitute a reservoir of highly skilled, talented and vigorous manpower whose energies and vision, if tapped and properly harnessed would lead us to the desired socio-economic upliftment and threshold of greatness... (Enegwea and Umoden 1993:113).

Buhari's military successor, General Ibrahim Babangida, was more enamoured by the achievements of individual corps members, stating that 'the numerous achievements of corps members, past and present, point to the fact that a technological breakthrough is feasible' (ibid.:157).

The NYSC directorate itself lists wide-ranging achievements – as would be expected. In its first decade the directorate sponsored surveys that pointed to high success of the scheme in terms of the impact on the participants and general assessment.[20] First is what the directorate regards as the 'less tangible' but ostensibly more crucial contribution of the scheme, which is 'fostering national consciousness and integration'. One such indication of that is taken to be the interest that parents and relations of corps members develop about the areas where their wards are serving, thus forcing them to 'think national' (ibid.:160).

Also, interaction among the corps members with fellow Nigerians of different ethno-cultural groups for one year is regarded as enabling them to 'appreci-

31

ate the basic similarities that exist between their culture at home and that of the host community' (ibid.). This is expected to lead to 'reduction in ethnic chauvinism and enable most corps members to develop a healthier and more accommodating attitude towards other groups of Nigerians' (ibid.). Inter-ethnic marriages resulting from the service year, [21] among others, have helped to build bridges and in 'harmonizing the diverse peoples of Nigeria', with the scheme acknowledged as 'perhaps the most realistic of all programs initiated since independence, towards the systematic Nigerianization of the nation's (120 million?) citizens' (ibid.:160–1).

At the 'tangible' level, the scheme in the last thirty years has made major contributions in the areas of manpower supply, education (the sector where about 70 per cent of the corps members perform their primary assignment), healthcare delivery and rural infrastructure, technology, sports and the self-development of the participants (ibid.:162–80; Adebisi 2001:29).

These major contributions to the Nigerian state and society are acknowledged by media reports, which praised the scheme in its second decade as, among others, playing 'a unifying role among the nation's various ethnic groups … thereby promoting the objective of "One Nigeria"' with 'the cultural interaction … (becoming) a blessing' (Enegwea and Umoden 1993:176), while it has also helped in crucial ways in 'tackling skilled manpower problems' and preparing the graduates for 'self-reliance, employment and self-employment' (ibid.:177).

Some problems are also identified, however. These include inadequate monitoring of the corps members, the perennial under- or non-utilization of their skills, the discriminatory employment practices in some states where 'non-indigene' corps members are not absorbed into the workforce upon completion of their service and the almost certain prospect of unemployment that participants have to face after the completion of the service year[22] (ibid.:182–7). One major problem, which soiled the image of the NYSC directorate but has often been ignored in its official history is the huge corruption uncovered in the early 1980s after an inquiry, which led to the imprisonment of the military head of the scheme and its chief accountant. For an organization created to instill discipline in youth and train them towards national redemption, this uncovering of massive corruption was an indication that whatever was being preached was not shared by those entrusted with preaching it.

In spite of these problems, an assessment of the scheme in its second decade affirmed that on the whole 'on it (the NYSC Scheme) lies our hope of national unity, of patriotism, and of a generation of Nigerians untainted by the evils of tribalism, religious bigotry and indiscipline' (ibid.:192).

Current Issues

In some ways, contemporary times are comparable to the historical conjuncture that necessitated the NYSC in the first place. At the end of the Civil War, the Nigerian state was in desperate need of a new breed of Nigerians, 'untainted' by the conditions that provoked the war, and buoyed by the new national resolve to ensure peaceful togetherness, progress and national greatness. The almost complete loss of social concord and sense of oneness that was felt at that specific conjuncture in the national history was more or less repeated from the early 1990s. One major manifestation of this, as already stated, is the descent into unending ethnic and religious feuds. The other signpost is the political and social strife provoked by the annulment of the 12 June 1993 presidential election won by Moshood Kashimawo Abiola, a southerner, which subsequently became a point of widespread anger and disaffection.

Even though most commentators overlook this backdrop, *The Guardian* saw things rather differently. According to the newspaper:

> With the general social, institutional and moral collapse in the country, the NYSC has suffered corresponding setbacks in its orientation and effectiveness. The visionary concept that gave birth to the scheme had blurred under a collapsed society and its shambling and discredited leadership. As morality and integrity took leave of the nation, so the scheme, once a proving ground for the budding and vibrant leadership of tomorrow, replicated the decadence under which the nation reeled ... with the laudable aims and objectives of the scheme in limbo and its operation thoroughly bastardized.[23]

Thus, in the third decade of the scheme, new challenges have emerged, provoking new thinking that the scheme, 'the bond of unity',[24] had outlived its usefulness and that it should therefore be scrapped.[25] This climate of opinion led to an inquiry commissioned by the government into the continued relevance of the scheme. Basic to these calls for scrapping are two strands of argument: those who make the clamour based on their assessment of the socio-political terrain and those who draw attention to the administrative problems and financial crises in which the scheme has been embroiled.

On the latter, purely administrative solutions have been proffered as alternatives to the scrapping of the scheme. For instance, on this platform, one of the 'fundamental changes' proposed is that corps members would no longer be posted to state capitals. Instead, all would be sent to rural areas to 'contribute to rural development efforts, learn citizenship and come to appreciate how the vast majority of Nigerians live'.[26]

Under the new 'democratic' dispensation, those making the calls based on socio-political reasons have been more strident in their demands for the scrapping of the scheme – which, one commentator said is 'on the verge of collapse'.[27] One former corps-member rued the politically divisive events that have caused the loss of faith in the programme in these words:

> It is unfortunate that times are changing, that people are again becoming hyper-ethnically conscious these days and some public commentators are even advising that each Nigerian should move nearer his or her home base (Enegwea and Umoden 1993:109).

A major cause of this situation in the last few years was the introduction of the Islamic legal code or *Sharia* in most of the states in the north of Nigeria. The debate on this caused a major national rift, with the southern states largely staked against most of the northern states. This acrimonious debate necessarily affected the NYSC scheme, a major institution for national unity. Legislative Houses,[28] ethnic and cultural groups and Christian organizations in the south publicly disavowed the introduction of the *Sharia* legal code and affirmed that they would not allow their wards to serve in sections of the country which, as the leading Nigerian activist and literary giant, Wole Soyinka, argued, had 'virtually seceded' from Nigeria. The Christian Association of Nigeria in one of the southern states declared in a letter to the president:

> We feel not bothered if Moslems claim that *Sharia* is about their way of life and that they want to be ruled by it (*Sharia*). But we are emphasizing that it is not a Christian way of life. As such, Christians do not want and must not be ruled by *Sharia* in any way and in any state. We want (the president) to know that we Christian parents love our children ... that we sent them to universities and polytechnics to learn.... We do not want them killed or maimed on the altar of any Moslem legal code called *Sharia*.[29]

The Middle Belt Patriots told a similar story: 'It does not make sense to spend all one's money to train our children, only to send them on graduation to the slaughter house', telling their wards not to report to '*Sharia* states' for service until the resolution of the crisis. The Confederation of Igbo Students deplored as suicidal the 'insensitivity exhibited by the NYSC in deploying female corpers whom they kit with trousers as part of their official uniform to serve in *Sharia* states, where it is an abomination for a female to wear trousers'.[30] The Confederation said its position was based on a 'well-founded fear over the security of Igbo corpers posted to such *Sharia* (Northern Nigerian) states due to the palpable state of insecurity arising from the declaration of the *Sharia* law or the plan to declare the

Sharia law in such states'.[31] A commentator even asked that southerners and Middle-Belters should stop sending their wards to 'the abattoir's arena' because 'they are too young to follow the barbaric laws without falling prey'.[32]

Some pointed to the corps members – over twenty – killed in the orgy of ethno-religious violence in the north, concluding that the 'patriotic commitment and enthusiasm' that informed the scheme 'have come under severe pressure':

> These phenomena have had the consequence of putting corps members serving in areas other than their states of origin, especially in the North to flight. (These have) weakened the overall national confidence in the scheme, and undermined its potentials for concretely forging a nation out of the present Nigerian multi-nation state.[33]

It was evident with this that, as another commentator stated, 'the future of both the NYSC and the continuity of Nigeria as one nation looks bleak',[34] again re-emphasizing how entwined the scheme that was designed to solve the 'intractable ethnic prejudices and hate that characterize inter-ethnic relations in Nigeria'[35] was with the same conditions that it was supposed to transcend. A major reflection of the loss of initiative even by the directorate of the scheme in the context of the acrimonious national debate was that the director general of the scheme stated that the compulsory nature of the call-up would be side-stepped for those who wished to wait until the *Sharia* crisis abated.[36]

But there is another side to this account that brings out the paradox. There were many who decided to 'stand by their nation by going to states in the north … in order to keep alive the ideals of the NYSC'. A commentator responded to this category of youths by reaffirming the basis of the scheme:

> What greater sacrifice can one make for the growth of this country? By their resolve to go to any part of the country, even the *Shariarised* north, in order to serve, these youths have undoubtedly come of age. They have shown that they are responsible, capable, have a mind of their own and are uninterested in the political gain some people wish to make out of the (crisis).[37]

There were also many who, though aware of the 'danger' as expressed by their parents and ethno-cultural associations, were nonetheless swayed by the 'lure of the NYSC allowance', which had just been increased before their call-up. Given the dwindling prospects in the employment market, the scheme had come to be identified as 'the veritable stop gap after graduation before plunging into the unknown hazards of post-service's worsening labor market crisis':[38]

Consequently, the first one week at respective NYSC orientation camps in the *Sharia* states had witnessed reluctant participants, held hostage by dearth of income earning options, despite promises of alternative arrangement, especially by some South Eastern states.[39]

For this latter category therefore, the key issue was not patriotism, but economic survival. It is in the context of this historical conjuncture of worsening inter-ethnic and inter-faith relations and economic crisis that the contemporary NYSC has to be evaluated. Some correctly regard the fallout over the *Sharia* as a symptom of a deeper problem, the fact being that the NYSC has largely failed to live up to its founding ideal. In actual fact, its travails have provided an illuminating cameo of the larger struggles of the Nigerian state, most critically the elusive quest for citizenship.

This quest intensified with the coming of civil rule in May 1999. After thirty years, the programme (never mind the Nigerian state) appears to be floundering and in dire need of re-visioning. As stated before, the broad theoretical project in this article is to probe the interface between service and citizenship using the NYSC as background. The key questions underlying the research relate to the actual nature of the relationship between service and citizenship, how politics has shaped the dynamics of civic service in Nigeria, and whether the NYSC programme has enhanced civic engagement in Nigeria. The following section outlines how data was gathered and analyzed in the attempt to answer these key questions.

6

Method of Research

Study Approach

We were interested in determining the extent to which the NYSC has been able to promote citizenship in Nigeria. As a corollary, we were also struck by the impact that the larger political travails of the Nigerian state have had on the NYSC in its quest for improved civic engagement among a section of the youth. Accordingly, the case study approach was used in our evaluation of the role of national service in the promotion of citizenship values in Nigeria.

The Southwest socio-political region of Nigeria was the main laboratory for this report, although we also conducted a number of interviews in the northern part of the country, especially in Abuja and Kano. The southwest is host to the nation's former political capital (Lagos) and remains the centre of political engineering and social mobilization. It has a relatively better record in terms of educational achievement and a vibrant civil society, especially the press and pro-democracy movements. Within the southwestern region, two states (Lagos and Osun) were selected for the purpose of the survey.

Four criteria informed the choice of Lagos and Osun States. First, the study took one state each from the apex and lower wrungs of the ladder using socioeconomic, political and demographic indices. The study further used geographical spread by picking a state each in the coastal and interior areas. Thirdly, the relative history of the states was also considered, selecting one each from the first and last generation of states in the region. Finally, the intellectual depth of the state as defined by the presence of educational (tertiary institutions) was also considered; one each from the group of states was selected with high and medium level of education presence (defined by the number of higher education institutions sited there).

Lagos, Nigeria's former political capital city, has the highest population (an estimated 14 million people) and remains the economic capital with a huge concentration of business activities. It is also the hotbed of pro-democracy activism, the media powerhouse, hosting the nation's leading media houses, and also parallels the complexities of the larger Nigerian nation. Osun State, on the other hand, is one of the newer states in the region, with a smaller population (four million people), and a lower level of socioe-conomic development. However, it still retains considerable intellectual depth, being host to one of the country's foremost universities, the Obafemi Awolowo University (formerly University of Ife), Ile-Ife.

Data Sources and Data Analysis

The study drew on data from primary and secondary sources. The primary sources included questionnaires, focus group discussions (FGDs) and interviews. An open-ended questionnaire was used in order to measure and monitor specific responses as well as give respondents the relative opportunity to express differing opinions on certain questions. The questionnaire comprised nine different sections (questions) covering the respondents' understanding of and reasons for establishing the national service scheme; the relationship between national service and citizenship values, national integration and national identity; and the continued relevance of the scheme.

Other aspects included the respondents' assessment of, and reasons for, the overall performance of the scheme. Significantly, the questionnaire carefully used eight markers of citizenship values to appropriately simplify the relationship between national service and citizenship, clearly assess and measure the respondents' understanding of citizenship, and to see whether citizenship values were divisible and to what extent the NYSC was deemed to have promoted particular aspects. The seven parameters of citizenship values used by the research included: civility, social bond, community service and patriotism. Others were sense of belonging, trust and civic duties (responsibilities).

Between March and May 2003, a total of 100 questionnaires (50 for each state) were administered of which 90 per cent (90) were properly completed by respondents; thereby rendering 10 void. Two Local Government Areas (LGAs) were targeted in each of the two states for the administration of the questionnaire (25 questionnaires were administered for each LGA). In Lagos and Osun States, Oshodi/Isolo and Lagos Island, and Ife Central and Ife East LGAs were selected respectively. The respondents were both serving and former corps members, thereby providing the possibility of comparing the extent to which opinions could differ between the two groups.

The respondents were carefully identified and questionnaires administered by the primary researcher and a field assistant in places such as NYSC Camps, places of primary assignments, offices and schools. Of the total 90 respondents who properly completed the questionnaire, 60 were serving corps members while 30 were alumni of the programme. The questionnaires were analyzed using tables, ratios and percentages to identify trends that were subsequently elaborated upon in FGDs and interviews. Crucially, the data generated from the questionnaires were analyzed generally and proportionally with a view to understanding the similarity or divergence of opinions between serving and former corps members. This greatly enriched the study by providing a rare, important opportunity to see the extent to which opinions and attitudes about the programme changed or were reinforced over time, especially in post-service years. The tendency to hold similar opinions during and after the service year seems crucial to our understanding of the extent to which the NYSC could or does enhance citizenship values.

Two focus group discussions (FGDs) (one in each state) were organized to provide insights into some of the observed trends in the questionnaires. Organizing the FGDs was a huge task for the primary researcher given the diverse backgrounds and occupational differences (with the implication for time and availability) of the participants. In fact, in Lagos, the required minimum number of respondents was only achieved after three unsuccessful attempts. The FGDs involved between eight and ten participants (who were excluded from completing the questionnaires), including serving and alumni of the NYSC. The participants were also carefully selected to reflect the diverse nature of the Nigerian nation; participants were drawn from as many different ethnic, socio-cultural, occupational and regional backgrounds as possible. The FGDs were recorded on tape and transcribed to provide clarity and document responses.

Finally, in-depth interviews were conducted across the two states to generate further explanations, understanding and perceptions about the NYSC scheme, especially as it affected citizenship values. The target group included officials of the NYSC, serving and alumni members of the NYSC, academics and members of civil society at large. Every attempt was made to ensure that the target group for the interview was not involved in completing the questionnaire and FGDs. Though tracking down the interviewees was quite daunting, the researcher was able to fall back on a network of contacts previously developed as a former journalist and pro-democracy activist to arrange the interviews – though on a couple of occasions it was quite humbling to know just how reliable some of these connections were!

In addition to the many unstructured informal interviews conducted to gain a greater sense of the state of affairs, six in-depth interviews were conducted during the same period across the two case studies. Of the six interviews, three were recorded on tape and transcribed while for the rest we had to take notes in longhand following reservations from the interviewees (especially NYSC officials). The FGDs and in-depth interviews were particularly useful in understanding in detail particular trends observed in the questionnaires.

7

The NYSC: Meaning, Perception and Interpretation

A central component of the research is the perceptual gulf dividing former and serving corps members. Thirty years after the NYSC was started as a critical component of the government's post-Civil War reconstruction plan as well as an important pillar of nation-building, it seems important to determine the extent to which a common meaning, perception and interpretation of the NYSC is shared or otherwise, and the extent to which such variation or similarity conditions the attitude of former and serving corps members as well as the impact on the goals and performance of the scheme.

Table 2: The Meaning of the NYSC

	Total	C.S_	C.B_	N.I_	E.O.	C.E.	E.R.	W.O.T.	Other
FC	30	9	12	16	7	9	4	3	2
SC	60	25	24	36	8	13	6	5	1
Total	**90**	**34**	**36**	**52**	**15**	**22**	**10**	**8**	**3**

FC - Former Corps members; SC - Serving Corps members; C.S. - Community Service; C.B. - Compulsory Obligation to the State; N.I. - National Integration; E.O. - Employment Opportunity; E.R. - Employment Requirement; C.E. - Cultural Exchange; W.O.T. - Waste of Time

Table 3: Reasons for Establishing the NYSC

	Total	N.I.	C.E.	L.T.	I.E.	H.C.W.	Y.D.	P.E.	Other
FC	30	27	6	9	5	5	9	8	1
SC	60	56	12	11	16	18	23	9	–
Total	**90**	**83**	**18**	**20**	**21**	**23**	**32**	**17**	**1**

N.I. - National Integration; C.E. - Civil Ethos; L.T. - Leadership Training; I.E. - Interim Employment; H.C.W. - Heal Civil War Wounds; Y.D. - Youth Discipline; P.E. - Promote Exchanges

From Table 2, of the total 90 respondents surveyed, 52 (57.8%) saw the NYSC as a national integration scheme; 36 (40%) saw the NYSC as a form of compulsory obligation to the state; and a further 34 (37.8%) interpreted the NYSC to mean a form of community service. Still, 22 respondents (24.4%) equated the national service scheme with cross-cultural exchange and interaction among the diverse ethnic groups in Nigeria; another 15 respondents (16.7%) saw the scheme in a purely economic framework (as a form of employment opportunity to young graduates); and finally, another 10 respondents (11.1%) equated the NYSC with a form of employment requirement. Lastly, eight respondents (8.9%) thought the scheme as a waste of time and an unnecessary impediment to their career (educational and professional aspirations), while to a paltry 3 respondents (3.3%), the programme meant other things beyond those already detailed.

Furthermore, from Table 3, 92.2 per cent of the respondents identified the promotion of national integration as the reason underpinning the NYSC, while 35.6 per cent saw the need to make the youth imbibe a culture of discipline as the principal rationale behind the scheme. Another 25.6 per cent linked the NYSC to the socioe-conomic and political milieu in which it was established, thereby identifying the need to heal the wounds of the Civil War as the fundamental reason for the programme. This was closely followed by 23.3 per cent of respondents who saw the provision of interim employment as the basis of the scheme; 22.2 per cent saw the provision of leadership training as the core reason for the NYSC; and 20 per cent saw its promotion of a civil ethos in youth as the most important function served by the NYSC. Lastly, while 18.9 per cent of total respondents identified the promotion of cultural exchanges, especially in a culturally heterogeneous country such as Nigeria, as the underlying reason for establishing the programme, a paltry 1.1 per cent linked the programme to other reasons beyond those already stated.

The responses reveal that a large percentage of serving and former corps members see the NYSC in a nationalistic framework – as an instrument of national integration and nation-building. The scheme's ability to bring youth from diverse cultures, ethnic backgrounds and geographical zones together both in the orientation camps and places of primary assignment is seen as a vital structural resource for national dialogue. Moreover, at the orientation camps, corps members are lectured on citizenship education and ethno-religious tolerance, and exposed to the cultural practices subsisting in the immediate environment, often outside the region of origin of the majority of corps members.

However, a more detailed analysis of responses revealed that, of a total 52 respondents that saw the scheme in terms of national integration, 36 (69.2%) were serving corps members while 16 (30.8%) were alumni of the programme. A similar trend could be observed in the number of respondents who identified national integration as the basic rationale for establishing and sustaining the programme. Here, a total 83 respondents, 56 (67.5%) and 27 (32.5%) were serving and former corps members respectively. More revealing is the fact that a majority of the serving corps members completed their orientation camp training a few weeks prior to answering the questionnaire.

Yet, when a proportional analysis of former and serving corps members is undertaken, the picture only changes slightly. For instance, of the 30 former corps members surveyed, only 53 per cent identified the NYSC with national integration. Also, only 60 per cent of the total 60 serving corps members also identified the programme with national integration. Thus, when the percentage of former corps members is adjusted to the number of serving corps members, the proportion of serving corps members is only seven per cent higher than former corps members.

Still, the trend suggests an episodic shift in the meaning and interpretation of the NYSC to respondents. During the service year, owing to programme activities, many corps members shared the foundational (official) goals of the scheme. The sheer togetherness and the sense of belonging to a special social category (of educated youth), ostensibly yields a high degree of nationalistic emotion among serving corps members. Not unexpectedly, the meaning, perception and interpretation, and the level of commitment to the ideals of the scheme marginally decrease as the service year runs out and beyond.

This presents an important paradox as the foundational meaning and interpretation of the scheme is weakened rather than strengthened after the orientation camps and in the post-service period. This can be said to mirror a transition from the normative (ideal) to the practical (actual experience), which mediates the relationship between the social imaginary or civic imagination that the corps

43

members buy into when they join the service, and the limitations of this social imaginary or civic imagination – and what they are able to construct – which they confront as they end their service and face the real world. This contradiction is also valid in respect of the percentage of respondents who see the NYSC as a form of community service; an employment opportunity; cultural exchange; and a way of making the youth imbibe a culture of discipline.

While the paradoxical decrease in the meaning and interpretation of the scheme is acknowledged, a large proportion of respondents still share a common meaning, perception and interpretation of the NYSC. This observation is further exemplified by the fact that only 8.9 per cent of respondents see the scheme as a waste of time. Respondents still see national integration, among a variety of reasons, as the underlining rationale for establishing the NYSC.

8

The NYSC: Performance Evaluated

After undertaking a survey of the extent to which former and serving corps members share a common leaning and understanding of the national service scheme, it is pertinent to see how the respondents perceive the performance of the programme. To this end, respondents were first asked whether they think the NYSC had achieved its aims and objectives. Such objectives included, but were not limited to, the promotion of national integration, patriotism and cultural exchange, serving as a training board for future leaders, promoting a culture of discipline among youth and fostering social bond among others. Second, since a majority of respondents shared a common meaning and understanding of the NYSC as a tool of national integration, the research also sought to determine former and serving corps members' views on the performance of the programme in this regard.

Lastly, we wanted to discover the bases of the respondents' judgment of the NYSC by identifying the real or perceived reasons underpinning the ability or inability of the NYSC to achieve its goals. As such, respondents were asked to privilege one or more of the following factors affecting the performance of the scheme, including funding, ethnic diversity/division, political leadership, youth culture, state of the Nigerian economy and, lastly, the 'Nigerian factor'.[40] The 'Nigerian factor' adds an interesting dimension to the study for it represents a mythical, often real, belief about the inevitable failure, under-achievement or impracticability of initiatives and projects that have proved successful in other countries. It is a complex mix of ethno-religious, cultural and geographical, socioeconomic and political factors that operate at most, if not every, level of governance and across the private and public sectors.

Table 4: The NYSC and the Achievement of its Aims and Objectives

	Total	Yes	No	Don't Know
FC	30	8	18	4
SC	60	20	27	13
Total	**90**	**28**	**45**	**17**

Table 5: The NYSC and National Integration

	Total	Yes	No	Don't Know
FC	30	16	12	2
SC	60	35	15	10
Total	**90**	**51**	**27**	**12**

Table 6: Reasons Underpinning NYSC Performance

	Total	N.F.	FDG	E.F.	E.D.	P.L.	Y.C.	Other
FC	30	11	5	10	9	10	5	—
SC	60	44	18	30	21	25	6	3
Total	**90**	**55**	**23**	**40**	**30**	**35**	**11**	**3**

N.F. - Nigerian Factor; FDG – Funding; E.F. - Economic Factors; E.D. - Ethnic Diversity/Division; P.L. - Political Leadership; Y.C. - Youth Culture.

From Table 4, of the 90 respondents surveyed, 45 (50%), representing half of the survey population, agreed that the NYSC has failed to achieve its general aims and objectives. Another 28 (31.1%) offered a contrasting opinion and firmly gave the NYSC a pass mark, while 17 (18.9%) were undecided. In contrast, when asked about the performance of the NYSC in relation to national integration (from Table 5), 51 respondents (56.7%) thought that the programme promoted national integration, while 27 former and serving corps members (30%) answered in the negative. Only 12 respondents (13.3%) were undecided.

From the foregoing, a generational differential in responses is also evident. Of the 45 respondents who saw the NYSC as being a failure, 18 (40%) were alumni of the programme. The data become more important when a proportional analysis is done. The proportion of the alumni of the programme relative to the total number of total former corps members surveyed was 60 per cent, while it was 45 per cent for serving corps members. Conversely, alumni of the NYSC constituted 28.6 per cent of total respondents who judged the scheme as having met its set aims and objectives. Again, the proportion of alumni of the programme relative to its total that judged the NYSC to have achieved its goals was 26.7 per cent, while it was 33.3 perc ent for serving corps members. Moreover, the opinion expressed by serving corps members (who constituted a gross 71 per cent of respondents who rated the NYSC as being able to achieve it aims) was representative of the initially positive view that serving corps members had about the scheme.

The gulf between serving and former corps members illustrates the marked tendency for perceptions and opinions about the NYSC to, paradoxically, decrease or turn negative over time; thus the initiation period at the orientation camp constitutes the peak of the NYSC – the peak of the civic imagination or social imaginary of the possibilities of national integration. It should be added here that given their enthusiasm and inexperience, these corps members might be substituting, in their imagination, interaction for integration and thus see the very fact of the interaction promoted and provided by the scheme as ready evidence of integration.

Lastly, it is significant that at least 50 per cent of respondents scored the NYSC low in terms of its ability to achieve set aims and objectives, from Table 6; a majority of this (61%) identified the 'Nigerian factor' as the major obstacle to the programme's success. This 'factor' is in core ways connected even to the structures of the social imaginary, in that it forms the backdrop of the possibilities and limitations of the construction of a nationally integrated, united and strong country. Another 44.4 and 38.9 per cent also identified economic influences (often interpreted as bad economic situation) and political leadership respectively, as other serious reasons for the poor performance of the scheme. Other reasons identified by respondents as being responsible for the less-than-desired performance of the NYSC included ethnic division/diversity (33.3%); funding (25.6%); and youth culture (12.2%). Only three respondents (representing 3.3%) identified other reasons beyond those listed.

Interviewees and focus group participants revealed that even at the orientation camps, corps members were treated badly by officials and that the general organization and co-ordination of the entire process was poor. In fact, respondents complained of widespread corrupt practices and discrimination ('favouritism') along social and ethno-religious divides within and outside the orientation camps by both officials and the general public. The FGDs brought out a more nuanced understanding of the state of affairs. Given their experiences during and after the orientation, corps members queried the assertion that bringing people from different parts of the country together would automatically enhance national integration and foster cross-cultural exchanges and interaction.

In many cases, new friendships, groups and companionships were still formed along ethno-religious divides during and after the orientation camps. Most corps members who were posted to areas outside their regions of origin and who had different religious faiths were often not accepted in their places of primary assignment. Besides, the recurrent problems of religious clashes (intolerance), negative ethnicity and inter-ethnic killings, and the leadership crisis in Nigeria over the past thirty years lent further credence to the complaints voiced by respondents.

9

The NYSC and Citizenship Values: Any Link?

Central to this research is the extent to which the NYSC promotes citizenship values and, by extension, a civic imaginary, that is, a sense of *Nigerian-ness*. Does service (NYSC) enhance citizenship values as defined by the eight criteria including civility, social bond, community service and leadership, patriotism, sense of belonging, trust and civic duties (responsibilities)? Evaluating this linkage in Nigeria has become important in the light of the increase, especially over the past decade, in the level of ethno-religious intolerance, leadership crises and a huge slide into uncivil behaviour by the youth and the larger population in Nigeria. Closely connected with this is the question of nation-being (Nigerianness) – does service (NYSC) promote a positive Nigerian identity? Nigerianness is defined as dynamic integration and display of those positive attributes of citizenship including civility, patriotism, commitment to the country, and national as opposed to ethnic or sectional identity.

Table 7: The NYSC and Citizenship Values

	Total	C	S.B.	C.S.	LD.	PT	SOB	T	C.D.	All	None	Other
FC	30	4	7	12	6	9	5	1	5	6	2	1
SC	60	8	18	29	11	20	10	2	19	7	3	—
N/Total	90	12	25	41	17	29	15	3	24	13	5	1
G/TOTAL (+13)	90	25	38	54	30	42	28	16	37	13	5	1

C - Civility; S.B. - Social Bond; C.S. - Community Service; LD – Leadership; PT – Patriotism; S.O.B. - Sense of Belonging; T – Trust; C.D. - Civic Duties

Table 8: The NYSC and the Promotion of Nigerian-ness

	Total	Yes	No	Don't know
FC	30	11	18	1
SC	60	33	22	5
Total	**90**	**44**	**40**	**6**

From Table 7, of the 90 respondents surveyed, 54 (60%) agreed that the NYSC enhanced community service in youth. Another 42 (46.7%t) and 38 (42.2%) argued that the programme promoted patriotism and social bonding respectively. A further 37 respondents (41.1%) identified civic duties as a core component of citizenship values promoted by the NYSC. Besides, 30 (33.3%), 28 (31.1%) and 25 (27.8%) serving and former corps members equally identified leadership, sense of belonging and civility respectively, as the citizenship characteristics enhanced by the national youth service scheme. Finally, while only 13 respondents (14.4%) agreed that the NYSC enhanced all the eight parameters of citizenship values, five former and serving corps members (5.6%) felt that the NYSC did not enhance any of the listed citizenship values. Only one respondent (1.1%) held that the NYSC enhanced values other than those listed herein.

From the foregoing, the mandatory weekly community development programme built into the one-year service programme underlines the view that the NYSC enhances community service in youth. A day is set aside every week for corps members to undertake projects aimed at improving the socioe-conomic development of the immediate local government area. Some of the more common projects include road safety patrol, HIV/AIDS awareness campaign, and the construction of structures such as signposts, schools and primary health centres. This weekly service to the community is designed to facilitate a warm reception of corps members in communities as well as orientate the youth towards the idea of selfless service to the nation.

Yet, further analysis reveals the regressive trend in the responses of respondents. Among the 41 (when deflated by the number of respondents who argued that the NYSC enhanced all listed citizenship values) respondents who saw the NYSC as enhancing community service, for instance, only 12 (29.3%) are alumni of the programme, while the rest (70.7%) were serving corps members. When a proportional analysis of the respondents is undertaken, this is 40 and 48.5 per cent of former and serving corps members respectively. The trend runs through other parameters of citizenship values in varying degrees. Some former and serving corps members interviewed contended that the weekly community service was ineffective in reality as frequently there were neither adequate funds to finance community development initiatives nor adequate supervision by the NYSC officials. Corps members complained that the community development day has turned into a weekly holiday, another day for meetings and socialization by corps members.

Moreover, interviewees and focus group participants identified the serious socio-economic and political problems that abound in post-service years as reasons why even some of the modest gains of encouraging values such as patriotism, community service and civility recorded by the NYSC were compromised in post-service years. This explains why the acronym NYSC has been reinterpreted to mean 'Now Your Suffering Continues'.

Similarly, from Table 8, 44 (48.9%) and 40 (44.4%) respondents respectively agreed and disagreed that the NYSC promoted Nigerian-ness. Only six former and serving corps members (6.7%) were undecided on the ability of the NYSC to enhance the Nigerian identity. The same regression trend is evident as 11 of the 44 respondents who agreed that the NYSC enhances Nigerian-ness were alumni of the programme. The percentage is greater when a proportional analysis is done and the total number of former corps members (30) surveyed is adjusted to the total number of serving corps members (60). Proportionally, 36.7 and 55 per cent of total former and serving corps members respectively saw the NYSC as a vehicle for promoting a common, positive Nigerian identity. The diminishing trend is far more evident in the number of former corps members who disagreed with the view that the programme enhanced Nigerian-ness – 18 alumni (45%) compared to 22 (55%) serving corps members. When analyzed proportionally, 60 per cent of alumni of the programme, compared with 36.7 per cent of serving corps members, rated the NYSC negatively in relation to the promotion of Nigerianness.

In conclusion, serving corps members are observed to hold more positive opinions about the NYSC than former corps members. One crucial fact is evident from the foregoing data, that the more time people spend on, and after, the programme, the more negative opinion their opinion was about the programme, especially in relation to the enhancement of citizenship values and the promotion of a common, positive Nigerian identity.

10

The National Youth Service Scheme: Between Continuity and Discontinuity

After a survey of the perception and performance of the NYSC, it is equally pertinent to evaluate the respondents' opinion on the continued relevance or otherwise, of the programme. To this end, serving and former corps members were asked to assess the overall performance of the NYSC. Though this is similar to the evaluation undertaken in the section of this report above wherein respondents were asked questions pertaining to the NYSC and its aims and objectives, yet it is still important to reassess the overall performance of the NYSC with a view to knowing if respondents felt it was successful, partially successful or not successful. This question checks further the validity of the responses to questions that were asked in the earlier section. It leads directly to the final question on the continued relevance of the programme: do former and serving corps members feel the resources expended on the programme justify the results? How rational is it to continue or discontinue the programme if it has failed or succeeded in its goals?

Table 9: The NYSC: Assessing the Overall Performance

	Total	Successful	Partially Successful	Not Successful	Don't know
FC	30	4	17	9	0
SC	60	9	41	8	2
Total	**90**	**13**	**58**	**17**	**2**

Table 10: The NYSC: An Assessment of its Relevance

	Total	Yes	No	Don't know
FC	30	18	11	1
SC	60	40	17	3
Total	**90**	**58**	**28**	**4**

From Table 9, of the total 90 respondents, 58 (64.4%) adjudged the NYSC to be partially successful; 17 (18.9%) considered the programme not successful; 13 (14.4%) said that the NYSC had been successful; and only 2 (2.2%) were undecided. Of the 58 respondents who adjudged the NYSC to be partially successful, 41 (70.7%) were serving corps members while 17 (29.3%) are alumni of the programme. Proportionally, of the total 30 former corps members, 56.7 per cent argued that the NYSC was partially successful; 30 per cent declareD the NYSC to be unsuccessful; and 13.3 per cent rateD the scheme as being successful in its overall performance.

On the other hand, of the 60 serving corps members, 68.3 per cent rateD the NYSC as partially successful; 15 per cent gradeD the scheme AS successful; and 13.3 per cent scoreD the programME a failure in the overall assessment. Using the proportional analysis as the more important indicators of group behavioUr, alumni of the programme tended to have less positive opinions about the scheme compared to serving corps members (for example, 56.7% of alumni compared to 68.3% of serving corps members who adjudged the NYSC to be partially successful).

Besides, the proportion of former corps members who had negative opinions about the scheme was higher than those of serving corps members (30% of alumni compared to 13.3% of serving corps members who adjudged the NYSC to be unsuccessful).

More important, the analysis in general correlates sharply with the mixed result recorded from the evaluation undertaken above wherein 50 per cent of respondents agreed that the NYSC had failed to achieve its aims and objectives, yet another 56.7 per cent of respondents argued that the program promoted national integration. This appears to demonstrate that while respondents rated the NYSC low in certain aspects (such as inculcating civic ethos and a culture of discipline in youth), they still rated the programme high in other areas (such as national integration). Moreover, the regressive trend observable in previous sections is equally evident here as former corps members seemed to have more negative views and judgments about the programme, while serving corps members were more positive in their outlook of the programme. But to what extent does this indicate the respondents' judgment on the continued relevance of the programme?

From Table 10, 58 of the total 90 respondents argued for the continued existence of the NYSC. Another 28 argued otherwise, while 4 were undecided. Of those who argued for the continuity of the programme, 40 (69%) were serving corps members, while 18 (31%) were alumni of the programme. Though the percentage of former corps members was higher when adjusted to the number of serving corps members, the number was still lower than the total of serving corps members. On the other hand, while 11 (39.2%) of the 28 respondents who wanted the NYSC discontinued were alumni of the programme, the rest were serving corps members.

What is interesting, once again, is that the proportion of former corps members (36.7%) relative to the total number of former corps members, and serving corps members (28.3%) relative to the total number of serving corps members, who argued for the discontinuation of the programme, reinforces this regressive trend. Thus the alumni of the programme seemed more negatively predisposed to the programme than serving corps members, while serving corps members had more positive opinions of the programme than former corps members. Is it a case of socio-political and economic innocence in the serving corps members?

11

Evaluation

Former corps members noted that that the NYSC was a good initiative that had turned sour over the years. For one, the programme seemed to have become more exclusionary than inclusionary. For example, the age cap has been lowered from thirty to twenty-five to decrease the number of participants; and graduates of monotechnics and part-time courses hitherto eligible for the NYSC have also been barred from participation.[41] Although this could be justified on the basis of the poor economic growth and performance of the Nigerian state over the past twenty years, nonetheless it is contended that such exclusionary measures question the rationality and continued relevance of the programme as well as an implicit admission by the government of its doubtful relevance. In fact, the negative slide in the quality of leadership in Nigeria is also seen as a factual indictment of the NYSC. The scheme is seen as training bad leaders (enhancing the 'chop-I-chop syndrome' – prevalent corrupt acquisitive spirit) and doing little to promote patriotism.

However, most critics still agree that a national service programme is an essential pillar of nation-building. The national service scheme in Nigeria is still relevant to the extent that it is redesigned and refocused to achieve its original goals. The problems of the NYSC, it is argued, parallel the foundational problems (ethno-religious and class divisions, corruption and bad political leadership, among others) of the Nigerian state.

Though the NYSC was established to resolve these key foundational problems, the programme has become another layer of the problematic Nigerian state. The NYSC could effectively enhance patriotism, for instance, only if the state discharges its reciprocal obligations to the youth. Until the larger crises of the Nigerian state are resolved, the NYSC will, at best, continue to provide formal structures for youth to meet in an 'holiday-like' manner without enhancing any citizenship value beyond the orientation camps or the service year at most.

Beyond Civic Imagination: A Contribution to the Critique of Service and Citizenship

Where national service is successful, some general outcomes are expected. Donald J. Eberly (1994) has articulated these outcomes thus:

> National service participants accomplish important tasks not otherwise being performed and they do so in a cost-beneficial manner. Participants in national service develop a higher self-confidence and increase their awareness of the needs of others. *National service promotes mutual understanding in a plural society.* Thus, national service often appeals to newly-independent nations as a way to promote a sense of nationhood among its citizens. National service is a vital form of experiential education. Participants learn from the experience with or without a deliberate educational component (emphases added).

He continues:

> *National service can be a unifying force among those who serve.* With the exce tion of the parent–child relationship, there is probably nothing that binds people together more strongly than working together in common cause. National service can fortify democracy because it is based on reality, not demagogy. National service programmes that *tap into strong central national values are the programs that tend to be substantial and more stable over time* (emphases added).

This is of course the ideal situation in which political, social and economic benefits accrue to the served and servers in a joint enterprise of communal/ national development.

The present work is premised on three assumptions: (i) that there is a necessary relationship between service and citizenship; (ii) that youth service in Nigeria has failed to promote a sense of citizenship among the youth; and (iii) that service can enhance citizenship only within a given socio-political context. The findings appear to confirm these hypotheses.

Any sociological account of citizenship – and its linkage with service – needs to consider three interconnected dimensions of citizenship (Roche 2000:217). The first dimension is the typical ideals and values of citizenship and of a community of citizens; the second is the socio-structural context that underlies citizenship as enabler and disabler of the capacities of citizens for development; while the third is the change in the nature of both citizenship and its structural context (ibid.). These are the dimensions within which we have tried to consider service and citizenship here. The failure of the NYSC to promote citizenship values in the youths towards the construction of a new *civis* in Nigeria is mainly a result of the objective and subjective conditions of the national socio-political context.

There is no doubt, as the survey, FGD and interviews reveal, that the scheme offers important social services, without which life in some rural areas in the country would have been less tolerable. It also helps greatly in fostering interaction among the youths and others across ethnic and religious divides. If the scheme were designed for surface-level citizenship training without its integrative ambition, perhaps it would have had a better assessment and would have been a success. As the survey and the FGD show, the scheme is largely regarded as successful on these counts. The overall failure is conditional on its more ennobling goals of ensuring national integration towards the construction of a greater Nigerian nation. And the failure has been conditioned by the emergent realities of the Nigerian nation and society.

As the inaugural chairman of the NYSC stated, two key questions were thrown up by these emergent realities: 'To what extent has the geopolitical development in Nigeria during the past twenty years affected the ideal? Is the nation still capable of recapturing the naïve optimism of the 1970s?'[42] The current Director General of the NYSC, Brigadier-General Walter Oki, reflects how the answers to these questions, taken against the backdrop of emergent realities, can oscillate between optimism and pessimism, and eventual acceptance of reality. Oki stated that 'there is so much mistrust and disharmony among Nigerians',[43] a gap which the NYSC has bridged, adding that 'this is one of the main things that has been keeping this country together as an entity'. However, Oki had earlier confessed in recognition of the increasing wave of inter-communal clashes that after thirty years, the NYSC is 'yet to achieve the desired national integration'.[44]

This confession is even more interesting when considered against the backdrop of the fact that most people in leadership positions in Nigeria today were former youth corps members. If Nigeria has not changed for the better and has in fact become worse, it is a clear indication that citizenship training through service has failed to achieve the onerous purpose of national integration and development. As a commentator has captured it, 'today, the idea of participation in the scheme no longer inspires patriotic interest as the old excitement appears to be fading away'.[45]

Why is this so? For a programme designed to repair society by nurturing a new breed of citizens through active service to fatherland, some fundaments are necessary. First is some necessary condition of community. As Perry and Katula, (2001:340) put it, 'sense of community reinforces the community problem-solving abilities (and) community cohesiveness'. In the absence of this, then, a sense of the possibilities of political community is crucial. On the heels of this social imaginary must follow sustained and positive political acts at the macro level that micro-level acts – such as youth service – will feed into, and which will nourish and reactivate these acts and such service. Without this resonance at the (political, social and economic) macro level, over time, isolated cases of individual and even collective service will not make citizens of youths who are, in the actual conditions of their daily lives, particularly in the post-service era, subjects who are exposed to realities that contradict all they have imbibed during the period of service.

The time and space interface is crucial to this argument. Many writers on service and citizenship are yet to fully realize the centrality of this interface. In the linkage of service and citizenship, it is not only the specific time and space of service that matters, but what happens after the practice of service and in particular contexts, both as a process of continuation of service and as the consequences of sacrifice that are observed in the spatial context. We need therefore to historicize our account of citizenship and service. As the Nigerian internationally acclaimed iconoclast and musician, Fela Anikulapo-Kuti, sang in one moment of intense frustration with the failure of his (musical) struggle for change in Nigeria, 'as time dey go, things just dey bad more and more' (As time goes by, things just get worse). So where the state and society decay continuously, as is the case in Nigeria, what can be the hope for a scheme that attempts to produce new citizens in a vacuum? Citizens imbued with the patriotic ideal and idea of citizenship, as duty cannot be produced in a vacuum. The objective conditions of the Nigerian state are such that the raison d'être of the NYSC is vitiated.

It also seems fashionable to mistake interaction for integration – as is evident in the responses of many of the respondents and the officials of the scheme. The facts in the last decade in Nigeria present a worsening case of inter-faith and inter-ethnic relations, and consequently greater disaffection and dissatisfaction with the Nigerian state. Since the return of democracy in 1999, the orgy of inter-ethnic and inter-religious clashes has claimed more than 10,000 lives, with several thousands more maimed and over 750,000 people displaced between 2001 and 2002. In 1999 alone, the police recorded 200 inter-ethnic and inter-religious clashes around the country. In 2003, the Delta State government spent ₦200 million (about $2 million) to maintain soldiers in the oil-city of Warri where three ethnic groups are permanently at one another's jugular. The Speaker of the Federal House of Representatives, Aminu Bello Masari, described what happened as 'near genocide' (Adebanwi 2004). Where 'citizens do not live in the republican style (with) a sense of community, of friendship and concord', service will not be a sufficient condition for the promotion of citizenship values (cf. Heater 1999:55).

A scheme for national integration cannot be considered successful while the country grows more divided. Adebanwi (2004) concludes that the evidence 'is an apparent indication that the Nigerian Union is seriously dysfunctional'. A popular essayist and scholar, Adebayo Williams, affirmed that the outbreak of communal/political violent clashes in virtually every one of the 36 states of the Nigerian federation, marks:

> *the absence of a founding and constituting normative order for the nation*, the lack of core values around which the political development of the country is structured, and the want of a system of deterrence which sustains and validates the core values with an almost abstract and impersonal rigour. Without the first, there is really no nation, only a conglomeration of contrary and mutually contradictory communities closeted in a colonial cage and clawing at each other to death. Without the second, a nation is stymied and critically disabled at source. Without the third, all social, political and economic exertions within the nation, all democratization procedures and development plans, are null and void because there is no code of conduct, no pan-national protocol to underwrite and sustain them (quoted in Adebanwi, 2004, emphasis added).

This comment summarizes the socio-political conditions that undermine the laudable goals of the NYSC and make it impossible to achieve them. In the absence of what Williams describes, the idea of NYSC helping to create citizens in Nigeria would, in the words of Ignatieff (1995), only constitute a 'noble myth' or 'fanciful lie' (Heater 2002:158) or one of 'the basic fictions which sustain' Nigeria.

In the inaugurating broadcast, Gowon essayed to 'drum into the ears of the youths of this country that (Nigerians') resources, energy and talent should be unreservedly directed and dedicated to those things which make for the realization and retention of the ideas which enable a nation to rise above its history and attain heights that would have normally been deemed unattainable' (Enegwea and Umoden 1993:256). The socio-political terrain presents this failure of the country to rise above its history of ethnic distrust, mutual recrimination and descent into violence that necessitated the service in the first instance. David Selbourne captures this situation variously as 'civic disaggregation', 'civic breakdown', 'extensive dissolution of citizen feeling', 'social and civic disorder' (1994:2-5, 13). Consequently, citizenship as 'a way to construct potential common ground, purpose and political language within the diversity' (Roche 2000:212) of Nigeria through duty has therefore failed to meet the enthusiastic objectives set for it.

Perhaps one useful way to proceed in the future would be to invert the question theoretically and see whether – and the likelihood is high – it helps us a great deal in dealing with data from developing or fractious polities, like Nigeria: Does citizenship influence service? If the question is posed in this way – (if) citizenship ! (then) service, rather than, (if) service ! (then) citizenship – we are likely to start from a departure point that is alive to the peculiarities of postcolonial polities with the interface of citizen and subject. If, as Olufemi Taiwo (2000:91) argues, in the case of Nigeria that there are no citizens in Nigeria' but only 'citizens of Nigeria' to point to a deep irony in which 'Nigerian citizenship lacks moral–ideological content' (100), that is, where legal citizenship has little or no value because it is neither respected nor linked to civil, political and social rights, then it might be improper to expect service to transform such a deep crisis that concerns even the ontological status of membership of political community.

In such conditions as this, we want to argue, it is only a resolution of the ontological status of membership that can presage and precede service, for already implied in the conception of service is the target – which ultimately is a 'community'. Consequently, in the context of youth service within a nation-space, this conception of community in which ideas of citizenship are rooted would be grounds on which the idea of service will first of all be based, before service can then, at the secondary level, begin to influence further enactment of citizenship – as duty.

Notes

1. 'A rare trait of patriotism', *New Age* (Lagos), Sunday/Monday, 5/6 October 2003.
2. While Borno State is in the north-easternmost part, the lady, Oluwayemisi Olomo, and her parents lived in Lagos, in the south-westernmost part of Nigeria.
3. 'A rare trait of patriotism'.
4. 'NYSC Boss Pleads for Corper (sic) Members', *Independent*, 12 November 2003.
5. Ibid.
6. Sherraden breaks out the components of this definition into phrases so as to understand them well. See his *Civic Service: Issues, Outlook, Institution Building*, Center for Social Development, Global Service Institute, Washington University in St Louis, Missouri, October 2001, pp. 2–3.
7. From Derek Heater, *What is Citizenship?* (Cambridge: Polity Press, 1999), p. 52.
8. (General Yakubu Gowon, Nigeria's Military Head of State (1966–75), during the formal inauguration of the NYSC Directorate, 4 June 1973)
9. 'Spotlight on NYSC at 25', *Daily Sketch*, 3 June 1998, p. 5.
10. *The Guardian*, 'Revisiting the NYSC Scheme' (editorial), 6 September 2002, p. 12.
11. In Enegwea and Umoden, 1993:104.
12. Indeed, university education at that point was subsidized by the Federal Government by up to 90 per cent.
13. The press had reported that N60 (sixty naira) – at 1973 rates more than $60 – would be the monthly allowance of the corps members. It turned out to be double that amount, that is, more than $120. See Enegwea and Umoden 1993:16
14. The first line of the NYSC Anthem. See Appendix 1.
15. See Appendix 2, the NYSC Pledge.
16. .'Linking Youth Service with Global Understanding', A Keynote Address by General Yakubu Gowon (ret.). www.utas.edu.au/docs/ahugo/NCYS/second/nys.html [accessed 17 January 2004].
17. There are discrepancies in the records of the actual numbers of participants. According to the first chairman of the NYSC Directorate, this figure was out of 2,757 initially called up and deployed: see 'The National Youth Service Corps: Its Genesis and Formative Years', by Adebayo Adedeji, in *A Compendium of the Natio-*

nal Youth Service Corps Scheme: Ten Years of Service to the Nation (n.d.), p. 32. But the second director of the NYSC, Brigadier S.K. Omojokun, puts the figure at 2,258. See 'National Youth Service Corps Scheme: Growth and Development 1975–1979', by Brigadier S.K. Omojokun, in *A Compendium of the National Youth Service Corps Scheme*, p. 52. Another chapter (2) in the same book stated the number as 2,364: see p. 85. Enegwea and Umoden (1993:25) agree with this figure. But William O. Iyizoba, quoting data from the NYSC State secretariat in Kaduna, put the figure at 2,340.

18. Ade Ogidan, '*Sharia* Takes Shine off Plum NYSC Allowance', *The Guardian*, 25 July 2000, pp. 29, 31.

19. Under this programme, corps members have made countless important contributions to the communities, including construction of maternity centres, dispensaries, bridges, incinerators, car parks, amusement parks, mosques, science laboratories, automatic power sirens, grain planters and applicators, radio transmitters, solar dryers, corn-shelling machines, etc. See Enegwea and Umoden, 1993:75–7.

20. See Appendix 3 for tables presenting the results of the surveys.

21. Some commentators professed the rather trite position that the scheme has 'fared well enough in fostering (the) much sought after unity (because) members have met and got married in the course of the program'. Emenike Bright Esike, 'NYSC: Which Way Forward?', *Post Express* (Lagos),28 March 1998, p. 7.

22. The serious economic crisis witnessed from the second decade of the scheme has led to a situation where corps members sometimes ask for extension by another year for fear of joining the widening pool of unemployed youths. See 'Unemployment Forces Corps Members to Demand Extra Year', *ThisDay* (Lagos), 29 May 1996, p. 1. One commentator even made the extravagant statement that 'the greatest (challenge) facing the NYSC today is no longer the issue of national unity and the concomitant of tolerance and peaceful co-existence, but rather graduate unemployment'. See Mohammed S. Alikali, 'NYSC and Unemployment', *New Nigerian*, 27 June 2002, p. 18. Another commentator argued that 'the scheme contributes to graduate unemployment in the economy since it provides cheap labour which is discarded annually'. See Oluwole Adejare, 'Time to Rethink the NYSC', *The Post Express*, 14 June 1997, p. 7.

23. *The Guardian*, 'Revisiting the NYSC Scheme' (editorial), 6 September 2002, p. 12.

24. 'NYSC, the Bond of Unity, Clocks 25', Gbenga Osoba et al., *The Punch*, Lagos, 25 May 1998, p. 11.

25. 'NYSC, Still Relevant 30 Years Later' (interview), *Daily Times*, Lagos, 5 June 2003, p. 23.

26. 'Refocusing NYSC' (editorial) *New Nigerian*, 28 March 2001, p. 4.

27. Idris Bida, 'Beyond the National Service', *New Nigerian on Sunday*, 31 August 1997, p. 7.

28. State Houses of Assembly, for example the Ondo State House, expressly told the indigenes of the state not to accept posting to northern states where *Sharia* had

been introduced. See Chuks Okocha and Funso Muraina, 'Don't Accept NYSC Postings to *Sharia* States, Ondo House Tells Indigenes', *Thisday*, Lagos, 7 July 2000, p. 3.

29. Lillian Okenwa and Joseph Musa, 'For Corps Members, Service without Consent', *Thisday*, 12 July 2000, p. 28.

30. Raymond Mordi, '*Sharia*: Igbo Corpers Confront Moment of Truth', *Daily Times*, Lagos, 12 June 2000, p. 28. The Zamfara State government had banned the wearing of trousers and all other related conventional dresses.

31. Ibid.

32. J.T. Bamkefa, 'Youth-corpers and Sharia States Posting', *Daily Sketch*, 24 May 2001, p. 11.

33. *Post Express*, 'NYSC and Sectarian Clashes' (editorial), Lagos, 21 March 2000, p. 8.

34. Lois Achi et al., 'For Corps Members, Service without Consent', *Thisday*, Lagos, 12 July 2000, p. 28.

35. 'NYSC and Sectarian Clashes'.

36. Mordi, '*Sharia*: Igbo Corpers Confront Moment of Truth'.

37. Lawal Ogienagbon, 'NYSC, Corps Members and the *Sharia* Threat', *Daily Times*, Lagos, 22 July 2000, p. 6.

38. Ade Ogidan, '*Sharia* Takes the Shine off Plum NYSC Allowance', *The Guardian*, Lagos, 25 July 2000, p. 29.

39. Ibid.

40. The 'Nigerian factor' has come to be identified as a constitutive anomaly in the Nigerian condition that subverts principles, ideals, regulations and virtually anything positive. At the extreme, it is regarded as an ontological irregularity seated at the heart of the constitution of the Nigerian state.

41. For more on this and other proposed changes, see the report of the technical committee on the reorganization of the NYSC scheme, 2002.

42. 'NYSC at 28: Integrating for Unity and Development', *The Monitor*, 16 January 2002, p. 24.

43. 'NYSC Has Cemented Nigeria's Unity – Oki', *Nigerian Tribune*, Ibadan, 13 May 2003, p. 16.

44. 'NYSC Yet to Hit Target, Says Corps Boss', *Thisday*, Lagos, 19 August 2002, p. 11.

45. Abayomi Adeshida, 'The Fading Glory of the NYSC', *Vanguard*, 15 September 1997, p. 5.

References

Adebanwi, W., 2004, 'Democracy and Violence: The Challenge of Communal Clashes', in Larry Diamond, Adigun Agbaje and Lanray Denzer, eds, *Nigeria and the Struggle for Democracy and Good Governance: A Festschrift for Oyeleye Oyediran* , pp. 327-348.

Adedeji, A., n.d., 'The National Youth Service Corps: Its Genesis and Formative Years', in *A Compendium of the National Youth Service Corps Scheme: Ten Years of Service to the Nation*, Lagos: NYSC Directorate Headquarters, pp. 18-47.

Aristotle, 1948, *The Politics*, translated by Ernest Barker, Oxford: Oxford University Press.

Azaro, S.R., 1993, 'The Ethics of National Service Implementation: Moral Dimensions of the Public Policy Debate', unpublished doctoral dissertation, Harvard University, Cambridge, MA.

Bandow, D., 1990, 'National Service: Unnecessary and Un-American', *A Journal of WorldAffairs*, 34(3):371-84.

Brav, J., Moore, A., and Sherraden, M., 2002, 'Limitations of Civic Service: CriticalPerspectives', Global Service Institute, Center for Social Development, WashingtonUniversity in St Louis, Working Paper 02, 12 July.

Chapman, B., 1990, 'Politics and National Service: A Virus Attacks the Volunteer Sector', in Williamson M. Evers, ed., *National Service: Pro & Con*, Stanford, CA: Hoover Institution Press, pp. 133-44.

Dagger, R., 2002, 'Republican Citizenship', in Engin F. Isin and Bryan S. Turner, eds, *Handbook of Citizenship Studies*, London: Sage.

Eberly, D.J., 1994, 'The Changing Face of National Service in the 20th Century', paper presented at the Second Global Conference on National Youth Service, held in Abuja, Nigeria, 10-14 October.

Eberly, D.J., 1998, 'National Youth Service in the 20th and 21st Centuries', essay prepared for the Fourth Global Conference on National Youth Service held at Windsor Castle, UK, June 1998, http://www.acys.utas.edu.au/ianys/essay.html [accessed 26 August 2002].

Ehrichs, L., n.d., 'Volunteering in Development: A Post-modern View', http://www.iyv2001.org/iyv_eng/research/articles/articles.htm

Enegwea, G. and Umoden, G., 1993, *NYSC: Twenty Years of National Service*, Abuja: NYSC Directorate.

Heater, D., 1999, *What is Citizenship?*, Cambridge: Polity Press.

Heywood, A., 1994, *Political Ideas and Concepts: An Introduction*. New York: St. Martin's Press.

Isin, E.F. and Turner, B.S., 2002, 'Citizenship Studies: An Introduction', in Engin F. Isin and B.S. Turner, eds, *Handbook of Citizenship Studies*, London: Sage.

Iyizoba, W.O., 1982, 'Nigerian Youth Service Corps: An Evaluation of an Attempt to Foster National Unity in the Face of Ethnic Diversity', unpublished Ph.D dissertation, Rutgers University, NJ.

Kalu, C. N., 1987, *The Perceptions of Ex-participants on the Effectiveness of the National Youth Service Corps (NYSC) in Nigeria*, Ph.D. Thesis, Ohio University, Athens, Ohio.

Menon, N., Moore, A. and Sherraden, M., 2002, 'Understanding Service: Words in the Context of History and Culture', Working Paper 02-1, St. Louis, Missouri: Center for Social Development, Washington University.

Momoh, A., 2000. "Youth Culture and Area Boys in Lagos" in Attahiru Jega, ed. *Identity Transformation and Identity Politics under Structural Adjustment in Nigeria*, Nordiska Afrikainstitutet: Uppsala, 2000

Moskos, C.C., 1988, *A Call to Civic Service: National Service for Country and Community*, New York: The Free Press.

NYSC, n.d., *A Compendium of the National Youth Service Corps Scheme: Ten Years of Service to the Nation*, Lagos: NYSC Directorate Headquarters.

Obadare, E., 2003, 'The Effects of National Service in Africa, with a Focus on Nigeria', paper presented at International Symposium on Civic Service: Impacts and Inquiry, held at George Warren Brown School of Social Work, Washington University in St. Louis, Missouri, 24–26 September .

Oi, W.Y., 1990, 'National Service: Who Bears the Cost and Who Reaps the Gains?', in Williamson M. Evers, ed., *National Service: Pro & Con*, Stanford: CA: Hoover Institution Press, pp. 81–103.

Omo-Abu, A.K., 1999, 'Ethnic Cleavages and National Integration: The Impact of the National Youth Service Corps in Nigeria', unpublished Ph.D dissertation, Columbia University, New York.

Omojokun, S.K., n.d., 'National Youth Service Corps Scheme: Growth and Development 1975-1979', in *A Compendium of the National Youth Service Corps Scheme: Ten Years of Service to the Nation*, Lagos: NYSC Directorate Headquarters.

Patel, L., 2003, 'Theoretical Perspectives on the Political Economy of Service', in Helene Perrold, Susan Stroud and Michael Sherraden, eds, *Service Enquiry Service in the 21st Century*, St Louis, MI: GSI.

Pawlby, I., 2003, 'What Should We Call «Civic Service»? A Commentary', in Helene Perrold, Susan Stroud and Michael Sherraden, eds, *Service Enquiry Service in the 21st Century*, St Louis, MI: GSI.

Perrold, H., Susan, S. and Michael S., eds, 2003, *Service Enquiry Service in the 21st Century*, St Louis, MI: GSI.

Perry J.L. and Kadula, M.C., 2001, 'Does Service Affect Citizenship?', *Administration & Society*, 33(3), July: 330–65.

Riesenberg, P., 1992. *Citizenship in the Western Tradition,* Charlotte: University of North Carolina Press.

Report of the Technical Committee on the Re-organisation of the National Youth Service Corps (NYSC) Scheme, 2002, Volume 1: *Main Report,* Abuja: Federal Ministry of Women Affairs and Youth Development.

Roche, M., 2000, 'Rethinking Citizenship and Social Movements: Themes in Contemporary Sociology and Neoconservative Ideology', in Kate Nash, ed., *Readings in Contemporary Political Sociology,* Oxford: Blackwell Publishers, pp. 209–37.

Selbourne, D., 1994, *The Principle of Duty: An Essay on the Foundations of the Civic Order,* London: Sinclair-Stevenson.

Sherraden, M., 2001, 'Civic Service: Issues, Outlook, Institution Building', Perspective Center for Social Development, Global Service Institute, Washington University in St Louis, October.

Taiwo, O., 2000, 'Of Citizens and Citizenship', in *Constitutionalism and National Question in Nigeria,* Lagos: Centre for Constitutionalism and Demilitarization, pp. 86–118.

Verba, S., Schlozman, K.L. and Brady, H.E., 1995, *Voice and Equality: Civic Voluntarism in American Politics,* Cambridge, MA: Harvard University Press.

Wyn, J. and Rob, W., 1997, *Rethinking Youth,* London: Sage.

Youniss, J. and Yates, M., 1997, *Community Service and Social Responsibility in Youth,* Chicago and London: University of Chicago Press.

Nigerian Newspapers Consulted

This Day, Nigerian Tribune, Daily Times, The Post Express, New Age, The Independent, Daily Sketch, The Guardian, New Nigerian, The Punch, and *The Vanguard.*

Appendices

Appendix 1: The NYSC Anthem

Youths obey the Clarion call
Let us lift our nation high
Under the sun or in the rain
With dedication and selflessness
Nigeria is ours Nigeria we serve

Members, take the great salute
Put the Nation first in all
With service and humility
NYSC for the noble youths
Make Nigeria a great nation.

Far and near we come to serve
And to build our Fatherland
With oneness and loyalty
NYSC for unity
Hail Nigeria our great nation.

Appendix 2: NYSC Pledge

In pursuance of our aspiration to build a united, peaceful and prosperous, hate-free, egalitarian society and a great nation and of our motto 'Service and Humility'.

I,...

(NAME OF MEMBER)

Member of the National Youth Service Corps .... (Year) hereby pledge to follow at all times the leadership of those in authority irrespective of their social and educational background and in particular I shall:

(a) At all times and in all places think, act, regard myself and speak first as a Nigerian before anything else;

(b) Be proud of the fatherland, appreciate and cherish the culture, traditions, arts and languages of the nation;

(c) Be prepared to serve honestly, faithfully and, if need be, pay the supreme sacrifice for the fatherland;

(d) Be well-informed about the history, geography, economy and the resources of Nigeria;

(e) Regard fellow Nigerians as my brothers and sisters and myself as my 'Brother's keeper';

(f) Have a healthy attitude to work and play. I shall not only be ready to work in any part of the country to which I am deployed, but also genuinely identify myself with the problems and aspirations of the people of the areas in which I work;

(g) Tackle difficulties and challenges in a disciplined and self-reliant manner, constitutionally pursuing grievances and properly channelling such for redress;

(h) See myself always as a leader who must give effective leadership by my transparent honesty and selfless service;

(i) Detest and shun bribery and all forms of corruption and nepotism;

(j) Be courteous and polite to all and sundry;

(k) Be obedient without being slavish; and

(l) Always remember the motto and strive continuously to live up to the ideals of the National Youth Service Corps during and after my service year.

So help me God ....

CORPS MEMBER

NYSC Call up No. of Corps Member ....

State Registration No. of Corps Member..

Date..
Sworn to at the National Youth Service Corps Orientation Camp.

This .... day of..................................(Year)................................

Before me..

CHIEF JUDGE

Appendix 3: The Impacts of NYSC Experience on Corps Members

Acknowledged effects by participants	Rating by participants (%)			
	4	3	2	1
1 - has provided opportunity for me to know other parts of the country better (%)	57	22	15	6
2 - has encouraged more self-discipline	36	45	16	4
3 - has increased my sel-reliance	47	42	8	3
4 - has increased my tolerance of others	36	38	20	6
5 - has increased my readiness to serve Nigeria in any capacity and in any part of Nigeria	37	35	20	8
6 - has made me more proud of Nigeria	33	31	26	10
7 - has increased my faith in the purpose of the scheme	26	45	20	9
8 - Others: Friendship with many others increased national outlookmore prudent in spending increased endurance readiness to work anywhere	66	20	11	3

Score: 4 (very much), 3 (much), 2 (little), 1 (not at all)

Corps Members' Assessment of the Achievement of the Scheme

Response	Awareness of similarities and common ties		Inculcation of self-discipline		National understanding and integration		Adaptability and self-reliance	
	No.	%	No.	%	No.	%	No.	%
Strongly agree	252	30.0	231	27.2	257	30.5	318	37.8
Agree	410	48.6	336	40.0	436	51.7	348	41.4
Disagree	126	14.9	203	23.9	74	8.7	126	14.9
Can't say	56	6.6	83	9.8	77	9.1	49	5.9
Grand total	**844**	**100.0**	**850**	**100.0**	**844**	**100.0**	**841**	**100.0**

Source: *A Compendium of the National Youth Service Corps Scheme: Ten Years of Service to the Nation* (Lagos: NYSC Directorate Headquarters, n.d.), pp. 134–5.

www.ingramcontent.com/pod-product-compliance
Lightning Source LLC
Chambersburg PA
CBHW021823270326
41932CB00007B/316